TRUMPS

DRAWINGS BY LARRY

Frankie Howerd

TRUMPS–
and how to come up

J. M. Dent & Sons Ltd
London Melbourne Toronto

First published 1982
© Frankie Howerd Scripts Limited and Victorama Limited 1982
Illustrations © 'Larry' 1982

This book is set in 12/13½ Linotron Melior by
Tradespools Limited, Frome, Somerset
Printed in Great Britain by
Richard Clay (The Chaucer Press) Ltd Bungay for
J. M. Dent & Sons Ltd
Aldine House, 33 Welbeck Street, London W1M 8LX

British Library Cataloguing in Publication Data

Trumps.
    1. English wit and humour
    I. Howerd, Frankie
    827'.914'08   PN6175

    ISBN 0-460-04550-4

Contents

1

Homily
from the Author

(if you'll pardon the word ... 'homily' I mean)

'There's no need to hang about waiting for the last judgement – it takes place every day.' So said Albert Camus. Now you're probably saying to yourselves, 'What the devil does Howerd know about Albert Camus?' Well, you're right – not much. But the point is that his remark, in a nutshell, goes straight to the heart of this book.

If, like most people's lives (mine included), yours has been beset by trials and tribulations, there is no need meekly to accept them. You can fight back. You may not always hold a winning hand but you've got to try to have a few trumps up your sleeve.

I try to be devious but I'm too transparent. There are, however, little streaks of cunning inside us all – the trick is to recognize them in order to create maximum havoc. If you can do so with your face wreathed in smiles, there is a chance you may get your own back without losing your popularity. Another useful ploy is to get the reputation of being a bit touched, of 'not being all there'. I've lost count of the number of times when, after doing something naughty, I've been able to play on people's sympathies by pretending to be half-witted. We've all got a trump card somewhere – it's just a matter of knowing how and when to play it.

If I've learnt anything from life, it's that only a fool or

an optimist seriously thinks that he or she can get through their time down here without falling arse over tit at some time or another. You can be as careful as you like. You can weigh it all up and know exactly where you're going and suddenly, hey presto, you find yourself flat on your back, gasping in astonishment at life's cruel tricks. It doesn't matter whether you're sitting on a bus, answering the door-bell, or just wiping the jam off the knife to open a letter from the tax man – round the corner Dame Fate's got a banana skin with your name on it.

From the electricity bill that's got the decimal point two places too far to the right, to the night out with the boys – when you prang the car getting into the garage, snap off the front-door key in the lock, cut your hand as you break the glass getting in through the kitchen window and then find that you've just broken into the wrong house – life's trials and tribulations come in all shapes and sizes. If we could all tell what was lying in wait round the corner, we could dodge it. But life's not like that. It doesn't signal its intentions in such an obvious way.

One of the most tiring things about showbusiness is not so much the actual performing, but what goes on in between – like most artistes, I've done a tremendous amount of travelling which of course, often means sitting among other travellers and joining in their conversation. But I find mixing with travellers can be very inspiring not only because I've come across many people who are as daft as I am and some, I'm pleased to say, who are even worse, but because I've overheard the funniest stories. It tends to make one more aware of what we call 'human nature' – especially its lighter side.

All the stories that follow feature ordinary people – and one or two poor devils like me, who find themselves in the public eye. The stories are of people coming up against what looked insurmountable odds – bureaucrats, faceless institutions, domestic crises, spiteful colleagues, overbearing bosses, bloody-minded neighbours, truculent transport officials – you name it. But they didn't bow down and allow themselves to be ground into the dust. Not on your nelly. No, these good folk made a stand. They took up the challenge. To use a well-known term from the ring, they boxed clever. They beat their opponents, often by playing their own game, and emerged clear winners. They came up trumps. Well, not every time – at the end of the book I have added a few examples of adversities that no trump card could overcome – not that another person couldn't have won through, just that the circumstances would have foxed most of us. And, occasionally, I've included an attempted trump – one that didn't quite succeed as planned.

However, while you're having a few titters at what follows, don't forget that you might come a cropper yourself in just the same way. I know I have, as have our friends in the stories you are about to read. But if they can bounce back and come up trumps, so can you. Don't start querying what bouncing has to do with cards, because you'll only exhaust yourself. Just sit back, pour yourself a drink and enjoy the scrapes that follow. And remember – the next time it could be you.

2

Red Tape

(or how to get unknotted)

I'd just about reached rock bottom in 1960 when the tax man, with unerring accuracy, hit me with a demand for thousands of pounds in back taxes. Like a fool I'd trusted others to take care of my tax affairs, and like fools they'd well and truly cocked things up. It cost me my little cottage near Reigate and an insurance policy just to keep afloat and I've been wary of red tape ever since.

I'd love to stand up as a champion of the individual against the forces of statute books, multinationals, the Inland Revenue, local government etc. but I'm not like that. Let others bear the standard, I'm happy to follow along in the wake. I've nothing but admiration for the man who cut his water rates by a quarter simply by insisting that the water board fit a meter to his mains supply, or for the lady in Hounslow who sent shock-waves through the tax office by filling in her tax return in her native language – Welsh. All it takes is a little determination and a fair degree of pigheadedness. With these two qualities any complainer will go far. I just wish I was that valiant.

Now this little story of mine may not have much to do with 'red tape' as it's generally understood, but as an example of how to pull rank, it shows the way to do it ... and taking this lesson one or two stages further, there's no earthly reason why you too shouldn't be able to come up with the right formula when you're dealing with snotty-nosed officials.

Picture the scene, then, if you will – Dennis Heymer, my mentor and right-hand man, me, Marty Feldman and his wife Lauretta (and a 'friend' of mine) let loose in Paris. We went on spec but the place was bulging with tourists and we had a hell of a job finding a hotel. When I told the others that I wanted to go to the Lido to see the world-famous cabaret, they thought I'd gone out of my tiny mind. The chances of getting into the Lido were about as good as yours truly being given a knighthood – though funnily enough, that's just how we did get in.

Our Lauretta isn't a girl to beat about the bush. She was on the blower as soon as I'd come up with the idea. In a marvellously languid and aristocratic voice she told the head waiter at the Lido that Sir Francis Howerd was in Paris for one night and was prepared to dine at the Lido, provided he, and his party of distinguished guests, were given the best table, and the best service. Now, despite the Revolution, the French are appalling snobs – they fell for this story hook, line and sinker. Naturally none of us had the right clothes to wear to the Lido, but that didn't matter. Lauretta and I went on ahead, being marginally the best dressed of the party. Bowing double, and walking backwards, the head waiter led us to the best table in the room. But the real fun started when Marty and the other two arrived. They looked such a shambles they nearly got turfed out before Marty had the chance to say that they were members of Sir Francis Howerd's party. Scarcely believing them, the waiter led them over and asked me to vouch for them.

'Oh yes,' I said haughtily, 'That's the mad millionaire, Viscount Feldman, his mistress and my valet. They may sit.' And they did, for one of the most entertaining (and expensive) evenings I've ever had!

Please speak ...

I don't know about you, but I reckon that people who have telephone answering machines are escaping from reality.

The problem I have with these machines is that they take away my whole line of attack. You may mock, but it takes me ages to work out in advance the best way of blowing my top, and when I find that a blasted machine is taking my message, it completely steals my thunder. The result is that Francis* is left floundering for words. An artist needs an audience, you see. When I first started in radio, I had to learn how to play to a dead studio, but that still doesn't stop me getting caught on the hop when I hear the words: 'This is a recorded message...'

That's why I take my hat off to anyone who can get their own back on these devices ... men like Mr Lionel Surridge of Kentish Town, who came up with a brilliant coup when he tried telephoning his local VAT office. He'd just been sent a thumping great bill which might as well have been the age of the VAT man's collective grandparents cubed, for all the relationship it bore to what he expected to pay. So he got on the blower and primed his guns. What did he get ... yes, you've guessed. When he heard the machine, like many people in the same situation, he slammed down the receiver without bothering to say anything. He had a cup of coffee and tried once more. Again the machine answered. After trying a third time and hearing the same: 'I'm afraid we can't take your call at present, but if you would like to leave your name etc. ...', it was obvious that he was going to have to write to the tedious little man who'd sent the bill.

He was dashing off to South America the next day for an important sales trip and the last thing he had time for was sending long letters to the Inland Revenue. Even so he got out his dictating machine and thought up a

*Francis, of course, is myself. I was baptised Francis Alick Howard. You may not think this worth a footnote, but I do!

suitably acerbic letter. He'd just said the 'Yours faith-fully' bit when he suddenly hit on an idea for making his anger felt.

Carefully rigging up his microphone and tape-re-corder Mr Surridge dialled the VAT office once more. Again the answering machine took his call. This time, though, he switched on his own tape-recorder and recorded the message being played by the answering machine. As soon as this had finished, Mr Surridge put down the telephone, stopped his own recording and rewound the tape. Once more he dialled the VAT office. Sure enough the answering machine came on the line, and when it told him, 'Please speak after the tone', he waited for the right moment and then switched on his own recording of the message and held the telephone receiver against the loudspeaker on his tape-recorder. The answer machine was now recording its own mess-age. He repeated this operation half-a-dozen times and then went off to lunch. Later in the afternoon he finally got through to the VAT office and was told that all internal lines had been reported out of order. He flew off to Rio the next morning a satisfied man.

Death by misadventure

Making no bones about it, I'm useless when it comes to being practical. If anything goes wrong, I'm stumped. But there comes a time when complaining about faulty goods to a supplier or a shop will get you nowhere. This usually occurs after the wretched machine has broken down once a week for the first eight weeks of your ownership, each time forcing your wife to rearrange her entire weekly programme to be there to let in the maintenance man.

Whether it's a cooker, a vacuum-cleaner, a fridge or a waste-disposal unit that packs up, you can be sure it will cause the maximum amount of nuisance for the mini-mum amount of improvement – at least it always has

chez Howerd. Sooner or later your supplier will throw his hands up in the air and tell you that you'll have to get on to the manufacturer to air your complaints. In other words he's cheerfully washing his hands of you and leaving you to get lost in the cavernous wastes of a large multinational corporation. What can happen at this stage is that you give up in despair, unable to face the months of writing letters to one official after another without ever finding anyone to take the blame. Don't panic, take a leaf (if you can afford the gesture) out of one successful campaigner's book.

Mr George Lough-Atkins from Southminster, Essex, came up against a brick wall when his washing machine refused to work and he could find no one to repair it. He realized that for once the size of the multinational manufacturer in question, Hoover, was to his advantage. He didn't waste time with an endless series of letters to the company. He decided to publicize the shortcomings of his washing machine in the most dramatic way he could dream up. He gave it a burial at sea.

The day after the fated product sank beneath the

14

waves, all the papers carried photographs of its sorry end. It was a pretty drastic, not to say expensive, form of revenge but at least Mr Lough-Atkins's trump gave him the satisfaction of nationally humiliating the manufacturers – something we all dream of doing. A simpler solution, perhaps, would have been for his wife to gather up all her young children's friends, cart them off to the shop that sold them the washing machine and let them loose with their sweets and ices. Nothing makes bureaucrats act faster than swarms of sticky kids creating havoc in their offices and showrooms.

How does your garden grow?

Not being a child of the earth, as you might say, my garden doesn't. But Mr Larry Siddington who lived beside the main Buxton to Bakewell road, had a garden of which he was justly proud, and each year he liked to introduce a new feature into the growing display of flowers and shrubs. One year he decided to tackle the dull corner of the garden that lay immediately alongside the road. He decided that some flowering shrubs would fit in nicely with his colour scheme and he carefully chose several which would come into bloom one after the other to provide colour all through the growing season.

As a public-spirited bloke Mr Siddington had the courtesy to inform the local council what he was planning to do, since his garden was cheek-by-jowl with their grass verge. To his amazement he got a letter back from the planning office saying that permission was refused.

Mr Siddington was hopping mad. He'd already gone out and bought his bushes. However, he had a sneaking suspicion that someone might come and check up on him, so he didn't ignore the refusal, as he felt strongly tempted to do, he sat down and replied to the planning office. This time he asked permission to plant *Atropa belladonna*, *Urtica diocia* and *Rubus rhamnifolius*. Permission was duly given and Mr Siddington went ahead.

Mr Siddington watched his new acquisitions grow with interest. He was right to have had his suspicions about the men from the council because one day he got a letter from them asking why there were weeds growing in his garden so close to the public highway. Mr Siddington wrote back to explain that he had been given permission to plant them, and he enclosed a copy of the letter that proved his point. Clearly someone in the office was unaware that *Atropa belladonna* is deadly nightshade, *Urtica diocia* are stinging nettles and *Rubus rhamnifolius* is the bramble bush on which blackberries grow.

When Mr Siddington reapplied to plant his original bushes he was given permission without question. Which just goes to show – when in doubt, blind them with science.

16

Paying for time

If you're unlucky enough to be drawn into the net of bureaucracy – a government department, a nationalized industry, the Inland Revenue, or whatever – there are plenty of ways to buck the system, especially if you can conduct a guerrilla campaign of long-range correspondence.

Firstly, always write – preferably barely legibly – rather than type. Never give a correct reference. Make sure you scribble wherever it says: 'For official use only. Do not write in this space'. If necessary, invent replies to letters you haven't received. If you get a threatening or objectionable letter from a bureaucrat, write back, attaching a copy of the letter, saying you thought he should know that some nut-case was writing to you using his name.

It's always a good idea, too, to stall on any payment you have to make until it becomes almost worthless. For instance, Nick Irving from Bromley got a letter from the Inspector of Taxes asking him for £54.78. Nick knew very well what this was for, but he decided to resist paying for as long as he could. So he wrote back to the Inspector acknowledging his letter, saying:

> Dear Sir,
>   Further to your letter and the outstanding sum of £54.78 that you seek, my records indicate that the sum owed is in fact £43.73. Can you please rectify your accounts and inform me of your conclusions?
> Yours faithfully, etc.

Nick was working on the well-tried principle that a bureaucrat will never settle for writing one letter when a dozen will do. Whenever the tax office wrote back demanding their £54.78 he simply replied that they'd got the sum wrong. This went on for over a year, by which time inflation had reduced the real value of what was being sought to almost the amount that Nick was offering to pay. So one day he just put a cheque in the post and totally confounded the system.

Illegal immigrant

Ever since my first trip abroad, courtesy of General Eisenhower and the D-Day landings, I've been an inveterate traveller, not that this has helped me get over my fear of flying. On one occasion I flew the Atlantic in such a state of panic that by the time I landed in New York, tranquillizers and a few drinks had rendered me almost speechless. The customs man went through my luggage with a fine-toothed comb convinced that I was drugged up to the eyeballs. I've always had a healthy respect for airport officials ever since.

Would that I had the cool of the New Zealand skipper who calmly sailed into his home port on a voyage from Fiji. As might be expected, the customs men came on board and, in the course of their inspection, they found a cockatoo under the captain's bunk. They promptly accused him of trying to smuggle the bird into New Zealand.

Not a bit of it, said the tar. While he was on passage, the cockatoo, misjudging its navigation, had flown straight into the main mast and fallen stunned into the cabin.

In that case, asked the men from the revenue, why was there also a large box of illegal bird seed hidden under the bunk? The captain had his answer ready, and played his trump. It wasn't hidden, it was stowed there because he and his wife liked to sprinkle it on top of their yoghurt. Naturally.

According to the rules

Outright strikes are bad enough, but in some ways they're not half as irritating as that other weapon of the modern age, the work-to-rule. It may be a rarely-used weapon but imagine the sort of mess we'd be in if everybody worked only according to the various codes laid down in their contracts. Working to rule seems to me to be a sure way of getting as little done as possible – but I suppose that's why they're used.

Anyhow, one brave soul, a Mr Eric Dutton, from Horsforth, Yorkshire, knew exactly what to do when his local bus crews went on a work-to-rule some time ago. He went on a work-to-rule himself – as a passenger.

Once he was seated on the bus Mr Dutton informed the conductor that he wanted to pay for his fare as laid down in the rule book which he had sensibly consulted. Before parting with his £10 note, he asked the conductor what proof he had that he was indeed a conductor. Then he demanded an assurance that his ticket was indeed a new ticket. Since the ticket cost less than 50p the conductor got a bit ratty. But Mr Dutton stuck to his guns and pointed to the relevant passage in the book to prove his point. The conductor finally gave him the proof he needed and grudgingly accepted the £10. But Mr Dutton hadn't finished by a long chalk.

Keeping a careful eye on the other passengers, he chose a request stop at which no one appeared to want to get off and rang the bell for the bus to stop. The driver duly pulled in and waited for someone to get out. But Mr Dutton stayed put. There was nothing in the book of rules that said that, having rung the bell, he was obliged to get out. He admired the view for a moment or two and then told the conductor that the bus could carry on again. The driver pulled out into the traffic once more and drove off.

Four stops later Mr Dutton rang the bell again. 'You again?' said the furious conductor. 'Are you planning to get out this time?'

Mr Dutton told him he was, but according to the rules he was obliged to remain seated until the bus was stationary. Finally, when the bus had come to a dead halt, George Dutton rose from his seat and walked carefully down to the back.

'Thanks very much,' he said. 'See you on the return run at 3.45.'

For no reason whatsoever this reminds me of the only occasion in a bus when I gave up my seat – not to a lady but to another man. I was sitting downstairs when a Scottish soldier boarded the bus, on a rather windy day, dressed in a kilt. The conductor said: 'I'm sorry, sir. There's only room on top.'

The soldier looked up the stairs and said, with great embarrassment,'I'm sorry, I'm not allowed to while wearing a kilt', so I gallantly gave up my seat and clambered upstairs, remarking whimsically as I went: 'In my regiment, we're dressed for anything.'

Protest march

I don't think I've ever publicly protested about anything. Once I had to make a stage entry in a parachute harness lowered from the flies, which got me into such a tizzy that when I finally landed, I thought I had been lowered by the flies. I stumbled in agony around the stage swearing vengeance on the clever Dick who'd dreamt up the idea. If he'd actually been there God knows what sort of public scene there would have been. As it was, the audience probably thought it was part of the act: 'Poor fool,' they must have whispered to themselves, 'if only he knew what a Charlie he looked.'

The trouble with airing any grievances in public, is that it's so easy to make a fool of yourself. Unless you can get your message across to the people who really matter, usually senior civil servants and government ministers, no one will take your protest seriously. And you could end up looking ridiculous into the bargain. So when in doubt go straight to the top.

The good people of Wooton Wawen, near Stratford, didn't take kindly to a plan to erect a giant incinerator near the secluded village and decided to air their protests to the man they held responsible, the Minister for the Environment, who was then Mr Peter Walker. However, they didn't travel down to London and waste time trying to see him. Nor did they start sending off angry letters to his department. They didn't even collect thousands of signatures in one of those impressive petitions that frequently get handed in to Number 10. They took a much more direct course. They found out where Mr Walker spent his weekends away from the cares of state and they descended on him one Sunday afternoon, all 500 of them. He quickly got the message.

Fortunately the inhabitants of Wooton Wawen were held back by traditional British instincts of peaceful protest, unlike the inhbitants of the Ivory Coast one day in 1950. A politician from France, Victor Biaka-Boda, who represented the Ivory Coast in the French Senate, set off on a tour of the hinterlands to let the people know where he stood on the issues, and to understand their concerns – one of which was the food supply. His constituents protested in no uncertain terms. They ate him.

The Tarzan touch

You don't have to live in the country to enjoy nature; in fact people who live in towns often have a greater appreciation of it than country-dwellers. There was a place near my home in Eltham, the Nine Fields, which gave me a great love of the countryside. I used to spend hours there, when I was a boy, and in my blackest hours the Nine Fields were always my refuge and consolation.

So I can easily sympathize with Jack and Enid Warren who had spent fifteen years of their married life sheltered from the view of the local sewage works by the magnificent elm that stood outside their house. They'd always looked upon the tree as being their own. Their kids had climbed it. Their cat had got stuck up it. They had sheltered underneath it from the hot sun on summer

21

afternoons and they had watched it shed its leaves each
autumn. It was theirs and they loved it.

Understandably then, the Warrens were dumb-
founded one morning when a council lorry pulled up
outside their gate and two workmen with chain saws and
ladders set about bringing down the elm. Mr Warren,
with an agility I've never possessed, grabbed his own
ladder and climbed into the upper branches of the tree
from his garden. Then he called to his wife to hand him a
length of rope from the garage before asking her to take
the ladder away again, leaving him marooned in the tree.

During the next six hours Mrs Warren sent up regular
thermoses of coffee and sandwiches in between tele-

phoning the local parks department and keeping the two council workmen sweet with tea and homemade buns.

The two workmen weren't to blame. They'd got a job sheet that told them to cut down the tree, but if Mr Warren was up the tree and wouldn't budge, they could hardly cut it down and risk going to court for injuring him. Besides, it was warmer in his lounge watching television.

In the meantime the head of the parks committee had been contacted and had had a series of urgent consultations with his officials. The outcome of these was that the Warrens' tree was removed from the list of those due for felling and Mr Warren was able to come down to earth again victorious.

That's what I like about democracy – it stops things being done.

Hand Luggage

Don't some of the modern regulations and formalities get up your nose at times? I often think it's easier to give up and take it lying down, but if you can score a point for common sense, the feeling of triumph is fabulous.

When US serviceman Andrew Nelson was told that he was being sent home to California after serving his stint in this country he didn't want to leave behind Felix, his cat. He made enquiries with Trans World Airlines to ask what they would charge for freighting Felix back to San Francisco and in reply got an enquiry from them; could he please tell them Felix's length 'from tip of nose to base of tail, his width across the shoulders while in a standing position, and his height from base of paw to top of head (not ears) whilst standing and looking straight ahead.'

Mr Nelson couldn't. Life was too short for that sort of caper. He tried British Airways instead – they were supposed to take good care of you. This time the airline passed the buck back to him and told him that he could work out the charge himself by following a formula which involved measuring Felix's crate; working out the cost of that by taking whichever total was highest; and finally adding the handling charges at both ends of the flight – about £15.50 all told.

Life was too short for that, too. Mr Nelson had a word in Felix's ear, gave him a good meal, bunged him into a bag and carried him onto the plane as his hand luggage for no charge at all.

The Biter Bit

Just occasionally one hears of a bureaucrat who strikes back – I'm not sure whether this is something to be encouraged or not. It's probably okay so long as he doesn't strike against *me*. However, Denis Healey, not long ago the Chancellor of the Exchequer, tells of one of his predecessors who found it difficult to compose his own after-dinner speeches and therefore delegated the task to a private secretary. After some years, the worm (if he'll pardon the expression) turned, and when the Chancellor was making his annual speech at Mansion House he read out as follows:

> 'My Lords, Your Grace, My Lord Bishop, My Lords
> Sheriff, Ladies and Gentlemen. The problem
> which faces us today is perhaps the most daunting
> which has ever faced our nation. Unless we can
> find a solution in the coming months I can see
> nothing but catastrophe ahead. There are only
> three possible ways of escape from the dangers
> now confronting us ...'

Then he turned over the page and continued the speech '... From now on, you're on your own, you bastard!'

And now, if I may be so bold:

THE RULES OF HOWERD

1) Never take any answer as final – until you get the cheque/the replacement/the public apology/the idiot sacked.

2) Don't be modest. Go public at the earliest opportunity. All the world loves a scapegoat, so put your knife in and twist it for all you're worth.

3) Remember that you're always dealing with a one-track mind. Get on that track yourself and, like the judo expert, use your opponent's flexibility to get your own way.

4) Don't fly off the handle and become abusive because it only provides ammunition for the other side. Appear reasonable and fair. Try to maintain a correct attitude when you write your letters, but slip in as many errors as you can. Wrong names, incorrect dates, cheques made out to the wrong body – any diversionary tactics like these can throw a spanner in the works and provoke extra work for the red-tapers.

5) As the saying goes, 'If you're going down, take one with you'. If you're doomed, the least you can do is drag down the cretin who's been the cause of your problem in the first place. Civil servants live in fear of bad reports that threaten promotion and the same is true of everyone else who hides behind red tape. Make a big enough fuss, they won't forget it. The only proviso is: try and do it *nicely*. Bad manners are too prevalent as it is.

3

Love, Marriage and the Family

(And do try and make it in that order.)

To follow the age-old pattern, boy meets girl. Girl gives boy the cold shoulder, or, alternatively, the green light. Boy gets carried away. Boy gets engaged and girl gets a diamond. Boy then meets in-laws. Outcome uncertain. Father gets shot of daughter. Mother gains a son. The building society gets another customer. Boy gets an overdraft. Boy and girl hear the patter of tiny feet. Family life begins another cycle. Time goes by. Rides on the cycle slowly decrease – if you know what I mean.

The story's been repeated since time immemorial. But with all that weight of experience to draw on we still manage to make some spectacular cock-ups in our everyday lives. Worse still, many of us find that the relationships which ought to be the easiest to manage often turn out to be the ones most full of pitfalls. For every remembered wedding anniversary, every breakfast in bed, every act of thoughtfulness by the kids, there are half-a-dozen domestic crises and disasters that threaten to throw the household into turmoil and curdle the milk of human kindness.

It doesn't matter whether the washing-up machine floods the kitchen with suds because someone's forgotten to put the waste-pipe into the sink; whether some relative you haven't spoken to for years suddenly turns up out of

the blue; whether the kids come home with half-a-dozen frogs that disappear behind the fitted cupboards – these are all stitches in life's rich tapestry, and every household needs to be able to do a few running repairs before the whole thing starts to fall apart.

I've always worked on the basis that safety in the home needs more than an eye for toys left on the stairs; it needs a whole list of useful phrases and excuses to pour oil on the troubled waters of every household and family crisis. More important still are those problems nearer the heart.

Let me tell you about the problems that faced me in 1944. As part of the grand army of liberation, Gunner Howerd found himself in recently liberated Europe along with a few thousand other lusty young chaps, most of whom were grabbing every available piece of crumpet in sight. Gunner Howerd, however, wasn't seeing too much of that sort of action and was feeling a bit hard done by.

Then Fate stepped in and presented me with more than I could cope with. Don't ask me how it happened but I found myself personally liberating the Hague! Yes, Scout's honour. I was in the lead vehicle in an army convoy and somewhere along the way the rest of the convoy got lost – the net result was that Gunner Howerd drove into the Dutch capital in splendid isolation to be mobbed by the entire population. God alone knows who they thought I was, but I wasn't going to let on. I had the time of my life; signing autographs; being carried shoulder-high through the streets; and more to the point, catching up on a bit of the fraternising that I'd been missing out on before. And I can tell you one thing – don't believe what you hear about Dutch girls. There's a lot more to them than Gouda and clogs.

Till death us do part

Jealousy is a terrible thing. That's why I'm relieved not to be a jealous person by nature. Heaven knows, I've had enough reason, but the milk of human kindness has always flowed through my veins, and I've always been too much of a coward to get into a serious wrangle. Usually, I just sit and sulk.

When love's the root cause of jealousy, there's little you can do about it, unless you can come up with a ruse like one chap I heard about. He was an impoverished young actor who fell madly for the daughter of a wealthy city gent. But her father didn't take kindly to the idea of his grandchildren being sired by a penniless thespian, so he packed the girl off to some swish establishment on the continent, well out of harm's way.

The actor always secretly hoped that his love would win through, but along the road the girl was swept off her feet by a titled rival. Their engagement was announced in all the best papers and there was nothing the poor devil could do. He wrote anguished letters, but they were all returned unopened. He even thought of going to the wedding and leaping up when the vicar came to the bit about 'just cause or impediment why these two may not be joined etc.', but he knew that he'd only be thrown out before the service got going. So he decided that any revenge he exacted mustn't involve him personally.

A couple of weeks before the wedding he was in the cast of a show along with several stunning young actresses. Apart from cheering him up immensely, this gave him an idea. He took one of these girls out to dinner, during which he hatched his plot.

On the day of the wedding the young actor stayed well clear of the action. After the service the happy couple came out of the church and paused on the steps to wave to the sizeable crowd that had gathered to see them. Then it happened. A gorgeous girl, weeping uncontrollably, dashed up the steps and flung her arms round the neck of the astonished groom, kissing him frantically.

'My darling! If you must go through with this ... be happy. But never forget our years together, never forget that when she tires of you, I will still be waiting!'

Then, with a final cry of misery, she wrenched herself away and disappeared.

It had cost the actor his week's pay to settle the score, but it was worth every penny.

Salmon-ella

Maybe you're one of those people who can't stop themselves from grabbing a bargain. But a bargain's only a bargain if you want it. And there are some bargains one could well do without, aren't there?

Noticing that tinned salmon was on cheap offer in the supermarket when she did her weekly shopping, Mrs Lizzie Gilbert of Colchester couldn't resist buying a couple of tins.

She opened the first one on the following Monday morning when she made her husband, Harry, his sandwiches to take to work. At the same time she put the rest of the salmon into Winston the cat's bowl. She knew that he'd enjoy it when he came in for his meal while she was out at her cleaning job.

When she got back at midday, however, and went into the kitchen, the cat's bowl was empty and poor Winston was lying dead beside it on the floor. Poor old Lizzie was in a right old tizzy (yes, dear, poetry too!) She dashed to the phone and rang her husband's boss. Immediately her mind filled with visions of Harry keeling over his lathe, clutching his guts.

'Mr Standish', she screamed down the phone, 'can you tell Harry not to touch his sandwiches. The cat's just eaten some of the salmon and died!'

'Right you are,' said the manager, 'I'll see Harry's okay, and then I'll call you back.'

The phone rang a few minutes later and Harry's boss said that he'd had a couple of the sandwiches during his tea-break, but an ambulance was on its way and they'd have him at the hospital in no time at all. He also offered to get a taxi for Lizzie, on the firm, to take her down to the hospital.

Meanwhile Harry, who'd been quietly getting on with his work, suddenly found himself whisked into casualty where his stomach was pumped out, while people in white coats fussed about giving him blood transfusions and drips. Then he was rushed off to intensive care where he was kept under sedation. Not even Lizzie was allowed to see him.

She went home, worried and worn out. A nice refreshing cup of tea was what she needed and she was just putting the kettle on when there was a knock at the back door and the milkman stuck his head round.

'I'm very sorry about Winston,' he said.

'How did you find out?' asked Mrs Gilbert.

'He ran straight out in front of me, see. I slammed on the brakes, but he was going so quick he didn't stand a chance. He couldn't have felt anything, mind. Didn't you find my note? The point is, I'd rather it didn't get back to the dairy – could make things a bit awkward for me if it did. Would you take a tenner and the odd bottle on the quiet now and then, if we said no more about it?'

'Only if it doesn't put you out,' said Mrs Gilbert trying to sound more generous than relieved.'He was getting on a bit anyhow. But don't worry, your secret's safe with me.'

Casual wear

I must admit to never having been a flashy dresser, it's not really my style. In fact there are those who reckon I look best in a toga ... but then they just go wild at the sight of my gorgeous legs. I'll dress up when I have to, don't get me wrong, but I never worry about what people should or shouldn't wear, unlike some.

Margaret and her sister Rachel, for instance, had never seen eye to eye when they were children and when they grew up and married they drifted apart even more. From time to time they were forced to meet up and, when they did, sparks flew.

Their relationship wasn't made any easier by the fact that Margaret's husband, Tony, was a good deal more successful in his business than Rachel's good-natured but bumbling Ronald. (Familiar, anyone?) The two men, however, got on with each other very well and this only made the two wives more uppity.

Margaret and Tony lived in Surrey, but because of Tony's agricultural machinery business, they often visited farming shows, and periodically they ventured into the part of Shropshire where Rachel lived. So one evening they were invited to have dinner with Rachel and Ron on their way up to a show the following day.

Although it was spring, the weather was still cold, and, used to muddy show-grounds and draughty marquees, Margaret was warmly clad in tweeds (on top that is – her undies were and are her own business). She also happened to be wearing the beautiful diamond brooch that Tony had given her for Christmas.

Rachel greeted them icily at the door but Ron was there with generous drinks and a warm fire. The two men got stuck into discussing direct drilling (a farm term, I hasten to add) while the two sisters went upstairs to freshen up. Rachel eyed Margaret's brooch and then scathingly remarked: 'You know, darling, I don't think you should wear such a large piece of jewellery with tweeds.'

'I know, darling,' replied her sister, 'that's what I used to say ... before I owned one.'

(The film director Michael Winner, with whom I made *The Cool Mikado* in 1963, once got me like that, on our very first meeting. The first thing he said was: 'You must understand that I am a genius.' And while I was still trying to think of an answer, he said, 'Who makes your suits?'

'Eh?' I said, not following this abrupt change in topic.

'The one you're wearing is very badly made. That's what makes you look so fat,' said Winner (not called that for nothing).

God, how I wish I'd had dear Margaret's command of the bon mot!

Agony column

I've never been drawn to the idea of the mock-Tudor house in Surrey, wih the swimming pool, whopping gin and tonics and a succession of flash motor cars — I'd happily settle just for the gin. But if you do get caught up in that set, it's not easy to hold your own (no crudity intended), as Maurice Adams found.

When he entered his son's name for his old school he hadn't the foggiest idea that there was going to be a recession. By the time young Roger had been there a year the family business was in a pickle and Maurice was in a jam. The last thing he wanted was to let the boy down, but he knew that Founder's Day was going to be a bit awkward when he and Roger's mother turned up in their battered Vauxhall Estate.

So Maurice swallowed his pride and put an advertisement in *The Times* which said quite simply: 'Wanted for hire Saturday, 20 June, Ferrari, Maserati, Lotus or Aston Martin to raise son's status at expensive public school.'

Maurice's box number received a dozen replies from sympathetic readers and, what's more, on Founder's Day, he clinched the best deal he'd had for many a month over a cucumber sandwhich with the owner of a Bentley parked next to his 'own' flame-red Maserati.

Who says money isn't everything?

Love sickness

Lovesick as I may have been at times, I never got in such a state over the ladies like this poor – how can I put it – sod.

In 1978 the *Whitley Bay Guardian* reported that the course of true love was so bumpy for railway worker Barry Hitchen that he had given up any chance of winning the affection of one of his passengers, Miss Sheila Mindon, and had decided to do away with himself.

After a farewell drink to the world one evening Barry walked into the sea. The water was so cold, though, that he waded out and went home to do away with himself in comfort. After wiring up his easy chair to the mains he threw the switch and all the lights went out. Barry didn't wake up outside the Pearly Gates. All he'd managed to do was blow the main fuse. Further attempts met with the same dismal result. He tried slashing his wrists, but even after smashing his best mirror and using the shards of glass, he found that his cuts were not deep enough and that his arteries remained stubbornly intact. Hanging himself from the banisters proved useless, too, because the knot kept on coming undone. Finally he decided to send himself up in flames with the living-room cushions. But as soon as these were alight he started to feel uncomfortably hot and jumped through the window into the flower-bed. Barry clearly needed help and the obvious people to turn to late at night in Whitley Bay were the Samaritans. When he tried to ring them from the nearest coin box Barry found he wasn't alone. The line was permanently engaged.

In the end Barry Hitchen gave up giving up and went off to bed. He found that committing suicide was too tiring.

Of course the real problem with Barry Hitchen was that his heart wasn't in it. And his main mistake was that he didn't let Miss Mindon know his true feelings. A true trump would have been to dive under the next express while she was standing nearby – he might have had greater success and simultaneously saved his living-room suite.

Marriage rights

No one ever did propose to me on any 29th February, though I must have given every likely candidate plenty of opportunity. What a chance those girls missed! Now with this young couple things were quite different.

Jane and William had been going out with each other for nearly two years. They seemed a perfect match and everyone was expecting them to get married, none more so than Jane. But William never brought up the subject and at first she felt too shy to start probing (to coin a phrase). But as time went on she became more and more anxious that he wasn't going to pop the question. When the time of their second anniversary came round, William took Jane back to the Chinese restaurant where he had taken her the very first time that they had gone out.

Everything was just the same as usual. They were friendly and courteous to each other and they had a giggle over the menu trying to decide which of the fifty-odd dishes to have. But when William was giving his order to the waiter and asked Jane absent-mindedly how she preferred her rice the expression on her face changed and she answered him pointedly: 'Thrown'.

For richer, for poorer

It strikes me that there's one really big advantage in staying single – you're never likely to be faced with the miseries of divorce. Yet how often do you hear people putting that forward as a convincing argument. Perhaps I could turn my talents to marriage guidance work?

Mrs Gertrude Vickers was a teacher, who, one afternoon just before the start of the Easter holidays, got home to find a note from her husband, Tom, telling her that he was leaving her after eighteen years of marriage. Poor Gertrude was not amused. She'd had her suspicions about her husband for some time, but she'd no idea that things had gone so far.

Tom hadn't given any address and she had no idea of where he was. Two days later she got a letter asking her to send him some papers and a change of clothes. The address he gave was Margate and she remembered that he'd been doing a lot of 'business' down there in the last few months. She wrote back to him saying that she couldn't find the papers he wanted and she doubted whether he really needed any clothes anyway, if her suspicions were right. There was silence for three more days until the next letter came. This time Tom outlined his reasons for leaving and suggested that they should think about getting a divorce. He'd found another woman, he told Gertrude, and they wanted to get married as soon as possible. Right at the end of the letter he asked her to sell his car and send him the money.

The Ford Cortina was only fifteen months old and was still in very good condition, so it was worth a fair bit. Gertrude took it down to the local garage and showed it to the salesman who told her that she could easily get

over £2,500 for it. When she got home Gertrude wrote to Tom to say that she would advertise the car in the local paper.

The lucky man who was the first to spot the advertisement couldn't believe his eyes. Even if it was a misprint he was still willing to follow it up, so he rang Gertrude and found that the car hadn't been sold. He got directions to her house and shot round as fast as he could.

The car looked as good as the ad said it did. The papers all seemed to be in order and Gertrude was even able to show him the service sheets from the garage showing what work had been done to the car since Tom had had it. Still unable to believe his good fortune the man paid Gertrude the asking price and drove off before she had time to change her mind. But Gertrude was quite satisfied with the sale. She'd got the price she'd asked for and she posted Tom the fiver that afternoon.

Test of time

I've not had too much luck with auditions. There was one in 1939 which I passed with several thousand others, but the casting directors weren't too fussy then. Fortunately, on the rare occasions when first appearances *have* worked with me, I've hit the jackpot. But I've always envied the sort of smooth-talking beggars I met at my ill-fated RADA (yes RADA!) audition who manage to sail through life with well-polished aplomb ... people like young Nicholas Walker.

Nick, an aspiring actor, had never met Carol's parents when he asked her to marry him. But once he was accepted he was asked round to their house to be given the once-over. Carol hadn't said a great deal about her family or her childhood, mainly because they hadn't known each other that long. So Nick didn't know what to expect when the door opened and he was invited inside. The meeting seemed to go very well. Once Carol's father heard that he'd got a secure job with the bank, he dropped out of the conversation and left the rest of the interview to his wife. Carol tactfully left Nick and her mother in the kitchen after lunch to do the washing-up so that her mother could have a proper go at her future son-in-law.

Nick stood up to the questions about his own family and education pretty well and came out feeling pleased with his performance. As Carol's mother was making the coffee they were talking about his and Carol's age when her mother asked him coyly how old he thought she herself was. This was the $64,000 question, Nick thought. His future happiness could depend on the answer he gave.

'I've got several ideas,' he replied. 'The only problem is that I hesitate whether to make you ten years too young because of your looks or ten years too old because of your wisdom.'

His safe passage through life with his in-laws was assured.

Things that go bump in the night

We've been told that we mustn't drink and drive ever since they first appointed a Minister of Transport. But what about the equally risky hazard – drinking and getting home again unnoticed, not by the police but by the wife? If there's one domestic disaster which ought to be avoided at all costs it's being confronted by your nearest and dearest on the landing at three in the morning when you're swaying uneasily against the banisters while trying to open the door to the airing-cupboard without being heard.

It should go without saying that silence is of the essence. Does the door-knocker bang when you open the door? If it does, hold it gently while you push the door. Have you put the key in the lock? It's wasted effort if you haven't and you might pass out under the strain of trying to break in.

If you assume that your brain is having its work cut out just keeping you upright, don't overburden it by sudden movements. At this time of night you're not going to gain anything by rushing your entry. It's far better to move steadily from one step to the next, taking every precaution you can.

What's immediately inside the door – the dog? Push it open gently just to be safe. It may even be waiting there for you, so stand upright and be prepared. All safe? Shut the door, but turn the knob in the lock and then release it gently when the door is shut. That stops the deafening click as it closes.

Now for the ascent. Leave nothing to chance. If you think there's the remotest possibility that you'll fall over when you try to take off your shoes, sit down; in fact lie down if that's safer. Try to remember which stairs creak. Avoid these, even if you have to step over two at a time. You can hold on to the landing, if it's low enough, or use the wall to steady yourself, providing you don't collide with the pictures, or leave tell-tale finger prints on the paper. Of course, if you're really far gone, you'll have no choice. Go up on all fours.

It's amazing how the most familiar domestic geography takes on a totally alien form in the dark when you've

had a skinful. So try to remember – if you can – what you normally pass on the way to the bedroom. Feel gently for any obstacles and move to the bedroom door as if through a mine-field.

Once you've found it, stop again and take another breath. This is the point where you drop the role of a mountaineer and become a safe-cracker. Remove as much surplus clothing as you can decently shed. (The really canny boozer hides his pyjamas in the bathroom and gets changed in there.) Tie up your loose change in a handkerchief. Put your socks inside your shoes. Undo all your shirt buttons – this isn't the time for pulling the whole lot over your head in one easy movement – and make it easy to slip it off. In the same way undo your pyjama bottoms before pulling them on.

Then, when you're certain that you're ready (and it could take ten minutes to be sure) gently grip the handle, pull the door towards you to cut out as much resistance in the catch as possible and turn it slowly and delicately. As soon as the door's ajar, turn the handle back again with the same care.

Check that your wife is fast asleep before opening the door further and then move your clothes into the bedroom without moving your feet. With luck, and the door to support your weight, you ought to be able to pivot into the room on one leg and execute a smooth waltz so that you end up inside the room and still holding the door. Now you have to close it, just as carefully as you opened it.

This is the point when many lose their cool and, flushed with success, blunder into the dressing-table, ricochet off into the wardrobe, where they bang their heads, and finally lurch in agony across the bed stubbing bare toes and knocking the glass of water all over their dormant spouse. That's not the way to do it. If you've made it so far, you owe it to yourself to finish the job properly.

So, check that you're wearing your pyjamas the right way round (buttons at the front, maker's tag on the inside behind your neck), then creep towards your side of the bed like an infantryman going over the top. Even at this stage don't make a rush for safety. Your missus will be warm and snug in bed, but by this time you'll be perishing. So crouch down and massage your feet until they're warm enough not to wake her up if you collide as you get in. Then ease back the bed-clothes just enough to slip in and lower yourself onto the mattress as you would onto a bed of nails.

Since the whirlies can carry you away at any stage of the descent it's often safer to prop yourself up and spend the rest of the night in a semi-crouched position with the bed-clothes pulled up round you.

It's only fair to say that you're bound to disturb what the glossy mags call 'your partner' at some stage in this last delicate manoeuvre. But don't let this worry you. If she throws out her hand to see what's moving the bed, get your hair down against it, then give it a lick and make one or two audible pants, before making yourself comfy. If ever there was a reason for keeping a dog, that's it.

By now you'll be wondering where the trump fits in. Well, it's like this. One chap who often went out to club dinners and came home late, much the worse for wear, usually teetering about in the manner described, received his come-uppance in rather a painful way. On the night in question he crept in the back door and tip-toed up the stairs in the fond belief, of which only the drunken man is capable, that he was being as quiet as a mouse. His wife by now was wide awake and watched with interest as he attempted to put his clothes away in the wardrobe. Alas, the whirlies got him as he was doing so and he reached out to the sides of the wardrobe for support. Unfortunately he held on too tightly and fell backwards onto the bedroom floor still clutching the wardrobe. All his wife could see of him was his head and feet at either end and his hands flapping feebly at either side. She knew what to do in just such an emergency. She rolled over and went back to sleep till morning.

Being of sound mind

I think most of us would like to go out in a blaze of glory with a state funeral, the nation brought to a standstill in universal mourning, tributes in Parliament and lengthy obituaries in the top papers – I know I wouldn't mind a spot in Poet's Corner.

But if you want to make a splash when you go it's best to be modest and stick to your nearest and dearest. No one else is going to give a damn, because most other people don't even know of your existence. But if you've constantly suffered sneers and jibes for your term down here, there's no reason why you shouldn't enjoy a private titter in the hereafter. How do you achieve that? The WILL.

Most people have something to leave, if only debts (those can be particularly useful if passed to the most deserving of your relatives). But usually there are a few goodies to be handed out to the family – maybe the nest egg that's been tucked away since George V's coronation which suddenly comes to light and sets everyone's mind spinning with ideas of compound interest and fat profits.

However, assuming that the Almighty gives you a moment to write your will before calling you up to join Him, you can leave a sting in your tail that your least favourite relatives won't forget in a hurry. Obviously the more you have to leave, the bigger the sting can be. But it doesn't matter what scale you're working to, the strategy can be the same.

In 1917 a very wealthy Austrian lady by the name of Mathilde Kovacs sent her whole fortune up in flames when she burned her will just before her death, thus depriving her relatives of untold riches. Their crime? They'd made unflattering remarks about her cats!

Other benefactors have left their fortunes to pampered pets in preference to money-grabbing human relatives. In 1944 a New York lawyer left his pet pussy more than $50,000.

But the strategy that's always amused me the most is the one that takes a little time to sink in. It follows like this: '... I, whilst being of sound mind, do bequeath my entire fortune to my dead brother, Henry, to be disposed of to the charity of his choosing.'

That's vicious. It's below the belt. But it will make your final minutes on earth ones of more than usual anticipation.

If I may make so bold again, more

RULES OF HOWERD

1) If charity does begin at home, look after Number One as a first priority. No one else will.

2) In love there are no winners.

3) Don't let your kids be your conscience. You've been around a good deal longer than they have. What may sound perfectly plausible is really only childish naivety.

4) Blood is thicker than water. So are most of the relatives.

5) Marriage is a partnership, a process of sharing. Both partners are equally guilty in the eyes of the Lord and the neighbours. Don't be magnanimous. Spread the blame evenly.

6) What the eye sees the heart grieves. Be cunning, sly, deceitful, anything that keeps under wraps whatever you are hiding.

7) When things fall apart totally, remember that the law splits everything down the middle. Do the same. Give as good as you get – but nicely.

4

A Working Life

(if forced)

Given that we spend about a third of every day dreaming of appearing in rum adverts in the Caribbean or having nightmares about the mortgage rate, that leaves half of the rest of our lives devoted to the daily round, unless of course we're actors, in which case there are usually a couple more shows before shuteye! It's not surprising therefore that our working lives are littered with rows, doubts, pay freezes and non-stop vendettas against our colleagues and the men and women at the top.

The world of work presents some of the most insurmountable odds most of us ever face – especially if you haven't got any. If we think that sorting out problems at home is heavy going, that's nothing to the jealousies, suspicions, accusations and malice that we can come across in the other half of our lives, and believe me, in the theatre that's painfully true – I've played Scarborough.

Apart from anything else, our livelihoods come closest to the brink when we're at work. The opportunity to fling a well-aimed spanner in the already ropey machinery of our finances and so threaten our very survival comes far nearer an adversary at work than it does anywhere else. All it takes is a mean-minded boss or a right sod of a work-mate to start rocking the boat and it's not long before we're swimming for our lives, and usually going down.

Sadly many a good man sinks without trace – look at F.H. who *almost* disappeared for good ... no, stop cheering. One or two manage to grab someone else and take them down too. Only a lucky few manage to keep their heads above water and make it to safety.

You don't get any thanks from your work-mates either if you stand up for your rights and lose. Though I'm the first to admit that pulling the cat out of the bag will make you a hero in no time. Why do I admit it? Because I've been such a hero.

It was at the end of my first film, *The Runaway Bus*, which I made with Margaret Rutherford and Petula Clark. The whole thing was being done on a tiny budget, which meant that most of the action took place in a pea-souper of a fog in order to do away with the need for any scenery. We'd reached the last day of shooting, or to be more precise we'd got half-an-hour left in the studio, when the director, Val Guest, suddenly told us that the film had a running time of only seventy-two minutes. So what, you may ask. I'll tell you what. In those days a film didn't get into the West End unless it ran for at least an hour and a quarter, and we were three minutes short, with only half-an-hour to put things right. Even with my powers of mental arithmetic, I worked out that we'd got ten minutes to film each of the missing minutes in the can.

Then yours truly came into his own, and true cunning shone through the gloom. 'Get the phone-box' I told Val (I'd seen a property telephone kiosk ... no, not the one from *Dr Who* ... standing at the side of the studio). And while the technicians got it into position I hastily propped up my script on a music stand, just out of camera. So for the extra three minutes of the film, the bus-driver, me, made a frantic phone call to his old granny, just like one of the old monologues that I used in my acts years before ... something along the lines of: 'Hello ... How are you? ... Have you seen the doctor? ... The dirty old devil! ...' etc.

Anyhow, it did the trick and *The Runaway Bus* not only got into the West End, it made a fair bit as well!

Wrong number

I know that I've developed a reputation for coming out of a show – I don't mean being sacked, though I've had a few near-misses. No, I mean stepping outside the character I'm playing to share a few asides with the audience, and altering scripts – both of which have been grossly exaggerated (I've only done it to improve things – at least that's my humble opinion). In fact quite a few people say 'he makes it up as he goes along'. This, of course, is far from the truth, though I occasionally add bits of dialogue or rearrange it in collaboration with the writers; generally speaking, all these spontaneous asides are written and rehearsed. After all, if one has gone through arduous rehearsals with a team of actors and one starts altering dialogue and popping in unexpected lines, naturally the other actors would be terribly disconcerted. Even worse, they might retaliate and also start improvising. For instance, if I was leaving the room and the actor who was supposed to say 'All right' were suddenly to ask a question I'd be in a right old turmoil. I'd have to think up an explanation and if we went on like that all night we'd end up adding three hours to the play and be performing hysterically to one man left in the audience who was sound asleep.

Of course, even in the best-rehearsed shows mistakes do occur and often this brings out the best in actors – or the worst. The great American comedienne, Eve Arden, was playing a summer season somewhere on the east coast of the USA. The show had been doing good business and the cast had settled into what they thought was going to be a successful run. In brief, some of them had started to let their hair down. One night Eve was on stage with one other actor. She was in the middle of a long, important speech when the phone on the stage rang. Needless to say there wasn't a sound cue at that point. But being the actress she was, Eve didn't falter. She just stopped talking and turned to the actor, who was down-stage of her. The look on his face told her that he'd fixed up for the phone to ring, so she went over to it, picked up the receiver and answered the call. 'It's for you,' she told him and handed him the receiver. With the tables turned on him so adroitly, he blustered and stumbled through a pretty feeble piece of ad-libbing. Then, when he'd replaced the receiver, Miss Arden resumed her speech as if nothing had happened. And it was the actor who needed the only prompt in the show.

Quality control

For actors there is only one form of quality control – putting bottoms on seats. If you don't do that, you've had it. But at least as an actor you have some control over your quality of work. I wouldn't want to go through this sort of carry-on...

Eric Benson of Rothwell, Northamptonshire worked on the casting shed of a concrete construction firm. His job was to ensure that the different casts came out of their moulds in one piece and were safely transported on their wooden carriers to the main storage yard.

Until the company was taken over by a flash outfit from London there were no problems about Eric's work. But as soon as the new management took over, tea-breaks were cut, work quotas were raised and quality controllers started prowling round the works checking the dimensions of all the pre-cast components of everything from coal bunkers to garages. Each quality controller was issued with a red marker pen which he used to draw a circle round any blemish or crack he found. Any red mark automatically meant that that piece was substandard and would have to be replaced with another. It didn't take Eric long to realize that if their bonus scheme was going to have any meaning at all, he and the other lads were going to have to produce almost twice as many pre-cast components as they had done in the past. And naturally in their haste more errors occurred and so more of the concrete components were rejected.

As far as Eric was concerned the new bosses were just making quality control an issue for putting the screws on the work force, and he for one wasn't going to put up with it. It looked as if the only way Eric could get his own back was to play the management's own game. He bought himself a red marker like theirs.

Over the next few weeks he made a series of secret forays into the yard where components waiting for despatch were stored. These were the ones that had been passed and no one paid much attention to them when they were loaded onto the lorries and sent to the distributors. Most of them had already been paid for anyway. All Eric did was to mark the odd one or two with the tell-tale circle or cross.

It didn't take long for the customers to start ringing up asking why their goods were arriving with reject marks. Within a fortnight the quality controllers had lost their red markers and things returned to normal for Eric and his mates.

The ultimate programme

Computers? Give me a pocket calculator and I'd show you how to burn it out in five minutes. I belong to a simpler age – probably the stone one. No, you can keep your computers. Indeed, anyone who strikes a blow against them gets my vote, like this chap.

When he was told that a cut-back in estimated production the following year would lead to him being given the push, a computer programmer working for a large American corporation provided a timely lesson to all who don't want their departure from the ranks of the employed to pass unnoticed.

He was told that he would have to go at the end of the

year. For the final few months he worked like a dog and no one could have suspected the little ploy he was working up. He went to the office Christmas party as usual and even sent cards to his colleagues, and when the time came for his farewell party his head of department made a moving tribute to his 'industry'. He told the programmer how sorry he would be to lose his services and said that no one would forget the time he'd spent working with them. He probably never spoke a truer word in his life.

The department's work load had eased off just before the Christmas break and no one took much notice of the routine programmes that were fed into the main computer. It was then that our man struck. While he was feeding the computer with a series of standard instructions, he slipped in an extra one, scheduled for 31 December.

'Erase all records', it read.

Exam nerves

In case you're curious about my academic background, let me say at once that I haven't any. Okay, I won a place at Shooter's Hill School against stiff opposition, but even so, I reckon my approach to exams had much in common with young Geoffrey Field's.

Some people are good at exams. Some aren't. Some work for them. Others don't. Geoffrey Field fell into the second category in both cases. (Others are just plain terrified, like yours truly.) One day, at the start of another term, Geoffrey sat down to face two papers for which he should have been revising during the vacation, when in fact he was earning £110 a week brewing tea for a couple of 'electricians' he'd come across in a pub in Ealing.

Geoffrey hadn't exactly been a star student the term before either, and as he glanced over the questions, he realized that if he blew this exam he could be slung out at the end of the year.

A further look at the paper showed that if he put all he could remember into one essay he might just get through. But he was supposed to write two papers, and spreading his limited knowledge over both wouldn't have done either of them any good. While the others scribbled away Geoffrey sat and sweated.

Then he had a brainwave. He wrote his name at the top right-hand corner of half-a-dozen sheets of paper and numbered them from 7 to 12. At the top of sheet number 7 he wrote a few lines which read like the conclusion to the first essay. Then he ruled a line below that and started to write the one essay which he knew he could just about do. He was careful to hand the papers in with a throng of other students, so that the examiner collected them hastily without checking the pages.

When the marks were published Geoffrey did considerably better than he'd expected. Careful inspection of the paper when it was returned to him showed that the examiner had taken the mark for his one essay and doubled it. But if Geoffrey's trump had worked, so had the examiner's. At the bottom of the paper was a note that read, 'perceptive and well argued – have kept first essay as model for future use.' Geoffrey was pleased with his results but even more delighted to think that the essay he *hadn't* written had been so good.

Animal cunning

There's a delightful story told about one of the world's leading neurologists, Sir Charles Sherrington, who was conducting an experiment with monkeys. He decided to observe how his group of monkeys behaved when they were not under direct observation. So he left the room in which they were kept and a few minutes later tiptoed back to the door to look through the keyhole. Evidently the same idea had crossed one of the monkey's minds, for through the keyhole he found another eye peering at him. Forty-love to the monkeys!

Mail order

All actors, whether rich, famous, or not, obviously owe their living to the public. In other words, they perform a service. In common with other professions that perform a service for the public – waiters, porters, taxi drivers, bus conductors – there is one thing that we are all expected to be – polite. In the case of an actor, it helps his popularity. In the case of the others I have mentioned, it helps their tips. Naturally it isn't always easy to ooze charm and politeness, as in the case of this particular member of the public.

Mrs Grace Ramsey lived in a quiet residential hotel in Worthing, West Sussex. She was a widow whose husband had left her well-provided and she'd decided to spend her declining years being waited on hand and foot by other people. But she wasn't the easiest of residents – in fact she picked fault with virtually everything. She insisted on eating breakfast in bed, even at the height of the season when the kitchen staff were fully stretched in the dining-room. She always occupied the most comfortable seat in the lounge. And she never gave tips.

The staff had grown used to her and largely ignored her moans and groans, but when a new hall-porter arrived, his patience quickly ran out with the old woman. Joe Tomlinson had worked for many years in a leading hotel in Manchester and he wasn't prepared to be bossed about by a grumpy old hag, who couldn't even give him a tip when he helped her into her taxi or carried her voluminous shopping bags into the lobby.

Joe was sitting at home one evening after another difficult day with Mrs Ramsey. His wife was leafing through one of those large mail order catalogues that allow you to inspect the goods before you pay the money, and when she'd finished with it Joe picked it up and started to thumb through it. For some reason Mrs Ramsey drifted through his mind as he was looking through the section featuring lingerie. Then it came to him in a flash. He found one of the order forms in the back, tore it out and filled an order for a very racy set of undies, giving Mrs Ramsey's name and the address of the hotel.

Ten days later he intercepted the parcel and handed it to her in person as she came in from her morning walk. At lunch-time a very gruff Mrs Ramsey handed the parcel back to him and asked him to post it for her (she never, of course, posted anything herself). Joe took the parcel, but when Mrs Ramsey had disappeared into the dining-room he removed the letter she had stuck to the outside and substituted one of his own.

Mrs Ramsey had written a real stinker to the mail order company telling them that she would never dream of ordering anything so obscene as the enclosed garments. Joe's letter was milder. It said that some mistake had taken place and what Mrs Ramsey had really wanted

was a tea-cosy, two Royal Wedding dish cloths and a candlewick dressing gown.

A fortnight later a second parcel arrived and again Mrs Ramsey returned it to Joe looking very affronted. He slipped in another substitute order and posted off the parcel.

This happy state of affairs continued for another four transactions before the mail order company respectfully suggested that perhaps Mrs Ramsey would care to do her business elsewhere. She was in complete agreement with them. But after that she made a point of always posting her mail herself. She didn't want the hall porter to get the idea that she couldn't afford the contents of the parcels which kept arriving from the mail order company whose name was always clearly printed on the front.

One up for Joe!

Sour grapes

It doesn't matter how easy-going you may think you are, when someone else gets the job you reckon you ought to get, it takes some swallowing. Many was the time during my dark hours (years) when I'd have done almost anything to have been given work. What made things worse were the tantalizing little carrots that kept being dangled in front of me, only to be snatched away at the last minute so that I plummeted even further into despair.

In one moment of panic I took myself off to New York where I auditioned for a Broadway revue with Hermione Gingold – *A to Z* it was called. It was exactly the break I'd been hoping to get. When I flew back to London my spirits were riding high. A fortnight later they came crashing down again when I got a letter telling me I wasn't wanted after all. That's showbiz, you might say, but it wasn't what I said, I can tell you. I'd happily have given cyanide to whoever they cast in my place. But perhaps that would have been too obvious. It might have been much better to have had the cheek to do what one aggrieved actor did.

This young American actor had been trying for a part in Hollywood. He hadn't really got off the ground after four years in the business and this movie would have given him the break he'd been waiting for. But it didn't work out. The producer took a liking to one of the other hopefuls and cast him instead.

When the loser heard the result of the screen tests he wasn't just bitterly disappointed, he was angry as hell. The one who'd got the part had flown back to New York cock-a-hoop. His loser knew his address there and in his gloom and despondency decided to send him a telegram. It read simply: 'DISREGARD PREVIOUS WIRE' and was signed by the director of the film.

When the actor phoned his rival's apartment a few hours later there was no reply. He'd jumped onto the next plane flying west to Hollywood.

Internal memoranda

Even from my very limited experience of working in
offices before the war, first in the docks and then for an
insurance company, I never could see the point of all the
paperwork. All those endless memos pushed from one
office to another – really! That's why I like this blow for
common sense.

In an effort to improve inter-departmental communi-
cation the firm for which Andy Porter of Nuneaton
worked decided that written messages carried more clout
than those passed through the internal telephone network. Andy and most of his colleagues realized what the
real purpose of the scheme was. The men at the top knew
that they were coming in for some scrutiny from a
powerful group of shareholders and they were trying to
make the company look as efficient as possible.

In the past the memos that had been sent round were
to do with serious subjects like fire regulations, annual
holidays or the result of the social club darts match. Now
desks were piled high with trivial enquiries about ship-
ping schedules, orders, equipment specifications and
import procedures which had previously been dealt with
by word of mouth.

Andy Porter found that he couldn't get on with his
work properly because he was always being interrupted
by these blasted pieces of paper. So he took it upon
himself to get back to the old system and started sending
particularly ridiculous memoranda to senior employees
of the company, which read like this:

To: Mr Judson
From: Mr Porter
Re: What time is it?

To: Mr Godwin
From: Mr Porter
Re: Weather. Is it raining your side? Suggest
switching on lights.

To: Mr Wiggin

From: Mr Porter
Re: Boxing Day. Does this firm intend to refer to 26
December 1981 as Boxing Day? Or should we refer
to 28 December 1981 as above? Suggest we refer to
26 December 1981 as St Stephen's Day and forget
Boxing Day for 1981.

Andy's ploy caught on with a lot of his colleagues and
within six weeks of the memo system being introduced it
was done away with. No explanation was given.

Specialist treatment

The only time I was able to turn the tables on some of my
officers during the war was when I organized army
shows. Some of them were a bit stage-struck, I was their
producer, and by God I let them know it. They say power
corrupts. It certainly corrupted me – I was nearly court-
martialled for insolence. Some of these young officers,
however, weighed down with one or two pips on their
shoulders, were worse than me.

One obnoxious runt was serving as a lieutenant in
Germany (where I'd finished my time in the war with a
gorgeous *fraulein*). Everyone knew that he was a maling-
erer but he'd got round the MO and had been sent off to a
military hospital for treatment. As an officer he went to
the officers' wing, where he found himself with a lot of
men who were far more ill than he was. Whether he felt
threatened by them, or whether he was just naturally a
pain in the neck, the result was that he soon drove
everyone hopping mad, moaning and groaning for days
that he wasn't being given the right treatment.

He was mightily relieved therefore to see a new face
above a white coat appear at the end of his bed one
morning. The man in the coat studied his chart carefully
and then asked in the matter-of fact tones that spell the
word 'specialist': 'Would you turn on your face, Lieutenant, and take down your trousers, I need to take a rectal
temperature.'

The lieutenant didn't argue. At last there was someone who took his illness seriously. He did as he was told
and the 'specialist' slipped a greased daffodil into his
bum and made his exit. The lieutenant discharged
himself shortly afterwards.

Threatening letters

As I've said earlier, you've got to be cool-headed to be a
debtor these days. Yet it seems that the people with the
biggest debts are the ones who seem best able to continue
living on tick.

It's the sheer audacity of many of the big debtors
that's always held up as an example of the way things
ought to be done. Reginald Marst-Horman ran a small
business that did the donkey work for large advertising
agencies. They got the big contracts and then passed the
buck to his little organization which stuffed the thousands of advertising envelopes and stuck the millions of
free offers onto the products that were being promoted.
Reggie did pretty well out of it, and after one very
lucrative contract with a large meat importer he went out
and bought himself a new BMW and then went on a very
expensive cruise. Unfortunately he had not put much
into the kitty to cover the heavy bills he had collected
doing the work. When the bills started to flow in he
wasn't able to settle half of them. Most of his suppliers
were sympathetic and allowed him a little extra time, but
one man persisted in hounding him for what was only a
fairly small amount compared with some of the other
demands that landed on his desk.

The supplier finally threatened legal action unless
Reggie settled his account in full. Reggie wrote back to
him saying:

Dear Sir,
    I can't think what you mean by sending me a
letter like that.
    Every month I make it a practice to place all my

outstanding accounts in my waste-paper bin. Then I calculate how much money I have to pay them. Next, I pick out as many of them as I have money to pay.

If you are not satisfied with my way of doing business, I won't even put your bill in the bin next month.

And blow me down the man shut up and waited his turn. Maybe I should have hung on to my cottage near Reigate. It would have done nicely for my retirement.

Sugar and spice

Apart from some unpleasantness a few years ago in Scarborough with the management – they seemed to think I was a little rude at times – I've always enjoyed my summer dates by the sea. There's the fun-fair, the candy-floss, the sticks of rock and the sea-food stalls at which I used to gorge myself when I had a bit of free time and felt peckish. I'd always wondered how they got the lettering in rock – until I discovered this little gem.

Ever since dental caries made the headlines and vile little cartoon creatures on the tele-ads got to work on gleaming white teeth there's been a bit of a downer in the sales of seaside rock. Parents have tended to buy their kids toffee-apples instead of the old twelve inches of peppermint candystripe. Where are the golden days of giant sticks that took a week to demolish?

Understandably, anyone involved with making rock has had good reason to feel hard done by. The pay wasn't up to much in the boom, but now it doesn't even keep pace with the rise in BL shares, let alone inflation. You need skill and talent to make rock with letters that run all the way from the soggy, mangled end in your mouth to the dry bit still wrapped in cellophane at the other end. But no one appreciated this, and, as the papers say, the morale of the work force was low.

Then came the brave man from a leading manufac-

turer of seaside rock. A sugar-boiler and lettering artist by
training, he was a confectionery anarchist in spirit. Not
content with mumbling his discontent at union meetings,
or furtively discussing revolution in the bogs, our hero
made a lone stand for recognition. He added a composition of his own to over a thousand sticks of rock bound
for Torquay. And for a good bit of that summer kids were

sucking this and then asking their parents 'Dad, why does it say "Stuff Torquay"? Shouldn't it be the other way round?'

Discomania

In the declining years of music hall, when radio, and later television, were beginning to win the audiences, there were still those singers who seriously believed that they should have been getting a better deal than playing the Empire Weybridge, or wherever it was, twice nightly. Some of these old has-beens lingered on, still churning out the same rubbish that no one wanted to hear.

There was one who, for reasons of libel, shall remain nameless, who became a proverbial pain for one poor BBC producer of my acquaintance. This producer ran a record programme on the radio, playing what we used to call 'light music' – the sort of stuff which people enjoy listening to, and which, by definition, never gets a look-in on the Third Network. Anyhow, my chum was constantly pestered by this awful little man because he never played any of his records. As tactfully as he could, the producer pointed out that the records were so lousy that he'd lose half the audience if he tried. But the man wouldn't take no for an answer. He even wrote to *The Listener* to complain that he was being victimized.

In the end there was nothing for it. The producer got hold of one of the man's records and was all set to play it on one of his programmes, when inspiration struck. He took it home with him that night and carefully bored another hole through it, this time just off-centre. He taped up the original hole and inked it in to disguise it as best he could.

The following day the record was slipped into the pile of others in its correct position. The producer provided the programme presenter with a suitable blurb about the artiste, saying how there had been such a demand for one of his songs that they'd chosen this example of his unique voice.

The record was duly placed on the turntable and played. But being off-centre the modulations in the man's voice would have done credit to the sound effects in a Hammer horror film. The programme presenter let the record run to the end, but he made damned sure that none of the singer's other recordings were ever played, in spite of the calls from housewives, who said they hadn't had such a good laugh in months.

A life on the ocean bed

Many years ago when we still had a navy that ruled the seas and when battleships looked like ships and not like floating runways and helicopter pads, a navigational officer in the Royal Navy, who for obvious reasons prefers to remain anonymous, achieved certain notoriety. Now the minimum requirement to be a good navigational officer is to be able to keep the ship in the sea − but I expect you can guess what's coming.

His first court-martial came about after he'd managed to wedge his mine-sweeper onto a particularly jagged stretch of coast in the north of Scotland. He'd actually succeeded in ripping open the hull like a sardine tin for almost half the length of the keel.

Sadder and wiser, he transferred to a larger ship for his navigational climax. Setting course for Spithead he steamed out of the wrong breakwater on a falling tide and ran her aground so thoroughly that at low-tide a local tradesman was able to drive his horse and cart right round the ship.

At the court-martial which followed he delivered his evidence as convincingly as he could. Before passing sentence the admiral in charge of the panel asked kindly where the officer saw himself going next, to which all but the bravest would have said Civvy Street, sharpish. Not this man, though.

'I think the best place for me would be in a school for

navigation,' he replied. 'After all there can't be many instructors who can offer the first-hand experience that I've had.'

To give them their due, rather than falling off their chairs with hysterics, the panel deliberated amongst themselves, and sure enough the hapless navigator was transferred to a shore school, where he became a leading instructor in marine navigation.

Ours is not to question why

As you might have guessed, Gunner Howerd had a pretty varied military career. Apart from defending Southend single-handed with another terrified conscript, I spent a few worrying months at an Experimental Station, in Shoeburyness, then a more agreeable spell in another Experimental Station at Penclawdd on the lovely Gower coast not far from Swansea. But for all my time, I never really understood what we were doing, or why. Truth compels me to admit that neither did anyone else seem to know what I was meant to be doing.

Happily, when the American artist, Hugh Troy, joined the army during the Second World War it didn't take long for his rebellious spirit to start hitting out at military bureaucracy. Lt. Troy found that he spent more time fighting the war with a pen than with a gun. His days seemed to be filled with endless form-filling, recording the life of his detachment in the minutest detail. This was supposed to give him and his fellow-recruits a taste of command. It gave them writer's cramp instead.

Hugh Troy knew that all the forms were pointless. They were shipped back to the Pentagon and that was the last that was ever heard of them. Yet at the same time he knew that he couldn't refuse to fill in the form because it was part of his training. His only way of showing up the futility of it all was to hit back in kind. Lieutenant Troy decided to invent a form of his own.

There were flypaper ribbons hanging above the tables

in the mess hall and lots of dead flies stuck to them. Lt. Troy decided that Washington ought to know the details of the fly mortality rate in his camp, so he had a form of his own printed and every week he filled this in, identifying the individual flypapers with code numbers and giving the numbers of dead flies on each one, and sent it off to the Pentagon with the bundles of other reports and forms that were despatched each week.

He heard nothing about the flypaper reports for several weeks. Then one day a couple of his fellow-trainees dropped in and asked him about the flypaper reports. They explained that they'd been getting stick from Washington for not having filed *their* reports, and wondered if he knew anything about them.

Hugh told them that he'd been sending off his flypaper reports every week, and handed them a sheaf of forms. They soon joined him in his crusade. As far as he knew when he left the army, the flypaper reports were still being sent to Washington. Maybe they still are.

RULES OF HOWERD
(again)

1) Whenever possible beat your opponents at their own game. Stick to the rules and you'll point up their stupidity far more easily. Apart from anything else your opponents won't understand any other approach.

2) Learn to delegate blame. Anyone who's ever got anywhere has mastered this art.

3) Never vote against somebody else's pay rise. It could be your own next time.

4) Whenever possible go to the top. That's the furthest you'll get from the reality of what's going on.

I hope you find these rules that confront you from time to time helpful. After all, you can always ignore them – or even do the opposite. That might be even more helpful.

5

Social Encounters

(or even under the counters)

If we still lived in the trees, things would be much easier, wouldn't they? I mean, there wouldn't be any need for the polite formalities that we try to preserve when we meet strangers. Actors suffer from this more than most, particularly if they're as easily recognized as I am – and that's not vanity, it's more to do with what's been unkindly called my weary camel face. The sauce!

There are a number of people who have tumbled to the fact that I am trying to be a comedian and come up to me in the street or elsewhere for that matter, expecting me to be instantly funny, so I've had to adopt a ploy for dealing with them quickly. Before they have a chance to put a word in, I beat them to it by asking what they do. Instead of me doing all the talking, I let them get on with it. Then there's the added bonus that they all go away saying what an interesting person I am, and how I'm such a good listener!

Mind you, even though we're supposed to be civilized now, that still doesn't prevent people from having a dig at one another whenever they feel like it. But, in the same way, any retaliation you make has to be toned down, too. Much as you'd like to get at some nit with a bread knife, or kick them senseless to the ground, you can't do that – unless you're on the football terraces of course.

And speaking of uncouth slobs, after a couple of bottles of anything intoxicating, even the posh crowd in West End clubs can get above themselves. I remember going with my brother, Sidney, to hear Tony Bennett at The Pigalle one night. Most of the audience were there to hear Tony, but there was one group behind us who talked all the way through his act. They were French and they probably thought they were being frightfully blasé. In fact they were just a pain in the neck. And a noise.

Of course, they were drunk and every time the rest of us called to them 'shush' they shushed each other, so in the end there was a cacophony of 'shushes'! I'd even brought my superlative French (of which more later) into play and had tactfully said to them: 'Ceinture haute, s'il vous plait', which was a fair translation of: 'Belt up, please.' But they didn't even respond to their native tongue.

The racket got so bad that I was moved to get to my feet. Just as I stood up, the lights on the stage went out as one act ended. I couldn't see. Then a waiter standing beside me blew open a bottle of champagne and the cork ricocheted off my hooter. Instinctively, I shoved out my hand in self-defence and made contact with the end of the bottle, pushed it away and sideways, thus changing the waiter's line of fire. The net result was that the Frogs were showered in champagne. An unwitting trump, maybe, but I didn't let on. It had all happened in a flash and by the time the lights came back on I was sitting in my seat the very picture of innocence, my face wreathed in sympathy for the poor soaked chaps from across the Channel.

Gentlemen's Excuse-Me

Many stories exist about the great F. E. Smith, later Lord Birkenhead, but one of the best concerns his unauthorized visits to the Athenaeum Club which he found to be a convenient stopping-off point on his way back from lunch at the Café Royal to the House of Lords. Certain members of the Athenaeum thought this was getting beyond a joke as, day after day, the great advocate walked into the Gents, and they persuaded the club secretary to tackle him one afternoon. When he emerged from the loo the secretary nervously challenged him: 'Lord Birkenhead, are you a member of this club?' In that unique way he had of turning the tables on his adversaries, the great man looked around him, taking ın the Greek pillars, marble staircase and fine paintings. 'Oh', he said with surprise in his voice, 'it's a club as well, is it?'

The Last Trump

If this isn't the most extraordinary trump, it certainly qualifies as the 'Last Trump'. A Mr Robert Jobb of Durban reported in 1981 that he had decided to commit suicide and had walked to the top of a tall cliff, near the city, intending to throw himself off. You can imagine the thoughts going through his mind at such a time. Suddenly a man appeared by his side, gave his name as Mr James Parrott, and asked: 'Are you about to end it all?' Mr

Jobb nodded. Mr Parrott merely said: 'let me show you how it's done' – and jumped. Mr Jobb fainted.

Season's Greetings

Do you ever get Christmas cards from people you haven't sent cards to? If you're the sensitive type it can quite spoil your Christmas as you worry and fret, trying to work out what the consequences are likely to be.

Keith Humber was a travelling salesman for a firm that sold photographic equipment to shops. His concern was with photograph albums and developing paper. His trouble started when he took a large order from a new retailer in Stoke only to have the man cancel it a couple of days later without any explanation. Keith got merry hell from his boss, who thought that he'd offended the man in some way and thus lost a valuable client. It was as much as Keith could do to stop his boss from transferring him to another region and he bore a permanent grudge against the man from Stoke.

Every year Keith's wife, Mavis, kept the Christmas cards that they were sent so that she could cut out the pictures on them and use them for decorations the following year. When she got out her box of cards towards the end of November Keith took a dozen of the cards for his own use.

He found out the home address of the ex-client in Stoke and since he had access to a wide range of stationery he was able to match the cards he'd taken from Mavis with envelopes the right size. All he did then was to post the cards one after another from different parts of the country.

His ex-client in Stoke was mystified by the cards that kept appearing out of the blue from people he'd never heard of, including short accounts of how the family were and enquiring after children that he didn't have. In the end, after several sleepless nights, he felt certain it must be the family he'd met on holiday in Minorca the year before, whose names he couldn't remember. What worried him most of all was the thought that they might turn up out of the blue.

If found

Fortunately I've been able to keep out of the clutches of the *nouveaux riches*. You know the set I'm sure; big cars, smart houses, a few horses – that sort of thing. A lot of people in the business fall for all that – but not me, thank goodness. No! No! Not thank *goodness*! Thank lack of *opportunity*! As the bishop said to the actress, the chance would be a fine thing!

Mr Michael Spicer and his wife Penny shared my feelings. They were once invited to dinner by the wealthy new couple that had moved into the house just down the lane from their home in Mayfield, East Sussex. Their new neighbours, the Brown-Palmers, lived in great luxury. Michael never found out how Alistair Brown-Palmer made his money but when they left they'd been given a detailed account of how much he had and what he was doing with it. Their hosts spent the whole evening picking their brains about investing in Jersey, asking what they thought of a recent issue of government bonds, wondering whether it would be worth their while buying the vacant farm down the road to run it as a tax loss, enquiring if they preferred Martinique for their holidays to the Canaries, and consulting them on the merits of Aston-Martins over Maseratis – the usual topics of conversation in fact.

At first Michael and Penny thought that they were sending them up in an entertaining way, poking fun at themselves. But when it was clear that the Brown-Palmers were perfectly serious, they started to take exception. Michael and Penny had an overdraft, a large mortgage that they were having trouble paying off, two kids at schools they couldn't really afford and a clapped-out Peugeot that was about to fail the MOT. In a word

they found the Brown-Palmer's conversation insuffer-
able.

After the meal Felicity Brown-Palmer suggested that
she and Penny should have their coffee by the fire while
the two men went into the library for a brandy. Alistair
led the way into a room lined with beautiful oak shelves
and filled with expensive leather-bound books. Michael
loved books and he had difficulty in disguising his envy
of Brown-Palmer's collection.

'Of course I don't get nearly enough time to read,' his
host said languidly. 'But I get that chap in Ross-on-Wye
to keep me posted if anything interesting comes up and
then I bung a cheque in the post. He says they're a good
investment. I don't know if he's right, but they do cut
down the heating bills. Another drink?'

When Michael and Penny walked away from the
Brown-Palmer's at the end of the evening they felt as if
their previously happy existence had been neatly shred-
ded in just a few hours. The other couple were so
damned smug and self-assured. Michael and Penny were
envious and that made them feel even worse.

The following day Michael was in town when he
passed a shop that sold bric-à-brac. On the pavement
outside was a bookcase filled with books selling for five
pence each. Michael stopped and had a look through
these and he noticed that quite a few of them had come
from a private library, at least they all had bookplates
stuck inside the front cover saying 'This book belongs to
...', but the name hadn't been filled in. Looking at these
labels the germ of an idea began to form in Michael's
mind and he bought three dozen of the books.

When he got home he sat down at his typewriter with
a packet of sticky labels and typed onto them Alistair
Brown-Palmer's name and address with the following
note at the bottom: 'If found please return. £5.00 paid for
safe delivery.'

He stuck one label into the appropriate place in each
book and then spent a pleasant weekend taking the

family for a drive and leaving the books scattered all around the area. Over the next week Penny kept an eye on the lane and noticed several unlikely-looking cars driving up to the Brown-Palmers' house. One even stopped and asked her the way. The driver was a large man dressed in farm overalls with a savage-looking collie sitting in the back. He said he'd found one of Mr Brown-Palmer's books and wanted the reward. Penny could just imagine how he and Felicity were going to get on.

Quick step

Although I say it myself, I was rather a good dancer (if my memory serves me correctly) unlike Alan Hill who never fancied himself as a dancer, but who fancied like anything the girls who went to the dancing classes he attended. One evening he managed to get himself part-nered with a girl called Linda, whom he'd admired from afar for several weeks.

When the couples were told to get on their feet and take the floor for the next dance, Alan grabbed Linda's hand and dragged her on. The music started and they set off, colliding with other couples and getting all the turns wrong at the corners.

'Can't you hear the piano?' Linda asked sarcastically as they crashed into the stack of wooden chairs on their second circuit.

'Yes,' said Alan, brightly, 'but I never let it bother me when I'm dancing with someone as pretty as you.'

Mistaken identity

Getting people mixed up is exactly the sort of embar-rassing thing that I used to do when I was younger. Nowadays it doesn't matter of course. I'm half expected to make an idiot of myself. So when I do, even by mistake, it doesn't matter. Now with others it's different.

John and Amanda were on holiday in Devon staying

in a cottage that belonged to friends. John had noticed that the car had been playing up a bit and one morning after a heavy fall of rain Amanda couldn't get it to start when she wanted to pop down to the village to buy lunch. Anyway, the sun was shining so she decided to walk the couple of miles instead.

When she got back she saw a couple of legs sticking out from under the car and, taking the opportunity to get her own back for a few playful pinches on her backside, she bent down and squeezed the bundle at their apex. Then she went into the kitchen and to her horror saw John washing up the breakfast plates. The man under the car was a neighbour who was helping him with the repairs!

Amanda explained what she'd just done and was all for dashing out to apologize to the man but John told her to sit tight because there was no point in admitting what she'd done unless it was absolutely necessary. He hadn't seen her after all.

When the man failed to come in after ten minutes for his cup of tea, they ventured outside and saw that he was still lying under the car. He didn't answer when they called him so they each grabbed a foot and pulled him out.

'I got a sudden pain in my leg which made me bang my head on the engine,' he muttered in a daze rubbing a lump on his forehead. 'I must've passed out underneath.'

Wrong number

It's pneumatic drills that drive me potty, but to some people the blackest day in the history of science was the day when Alexander Graham Bell invented the telephone and in so doing opened the door to the source of their greatest annoyances, the wrong number.

If you're anything like as nervous and timid as I used to be, answering the telephone is a nerve-wracking business in itself, but lifting the receiver, giving your number and then being told that the caller has misdialled is the most awful anticlimax when you're all keyed-up and apprehensive. However, there are various ways of settling the score. I've found that people's responses depend largely on who's calling and what they want.

If you get a cheerful voice on the other end asking for Dave, for example, why not try a dramatic reply? Put on your best hysterical voice and scream down the phone: 'God, something awful's happening. Get off the line. Wait right where you are until we ring back', then slam down the phone. (If you've got a suitable gun nearby you could try firing a few shots before the phone goes dead.)

On the other hand if you get a man's voice asking for a girl, you can have much more fun. If you're a man answering the call, you can tell the man on the other end: 'Eileen's finished with you. I'm here now, so don't bother ringing back. See?' If you're a woman you can tell the caller, 'Eileen's up in her room with a client at the moment. Can you ring back in half an hour or would you care to make a booking for next week?

Alternatively you can do what I've done in desperation – lift the receiver and say in my best Jack Warner voice: 'Paddington Green Police Station ...' That soon clears the line.

Conversation piece

In my young days I found I could be quite a hit with ladies by using a little old-world chivalry and charm – it was in pretty short supply then. Now it's quite different. Girls these days are so independent and self-assured that most of the ones I fancy scare the living daylights out of me. The only compensation is that today's young men can usually fend for themselves, as in this instance.

A young man and a young woman found themselves the only people in their 'twenties at a party given by the young woman's parents – which isn't entirely surprising. Though attracted to each other neither was prepared to make the first move. They fenced with each other. Their conversation covered the usual topics; work; films; plays; the cost of rents in London; health food; etc. But beneath this ran a subtle sub-text in which each tried to score points over the other – love's old sweet song and little Cupid with his bloody bow and arrow interfering again.

Finally the young man started to give way and admitted grudgingly: 'Actually, you're not a bad-looking sort of a girl yourself.'

'I expect you'd say that even if you didn't think so,' the girl told him.

'That makes us quits, then,' said the young man bouncing back. 'I expect you'd think so even if I didn't tell you.'

Incognito

As a rule I'm pretty good about watching what I say. Only once have I kicked myself for having gone too far, and that was under rather exceptional circumstances – a private performance of *Variety Bandbox* at Buckingham Palace (yes, Buckingham, not Alexandra). Not that I put my foot in it then – Heaven forbid. It was the Queen Mother's (Queen Elizabeth as she then was) fault really. She was so warm and friendly that I completely lost my shyness and launched into a painfully long story about how I was once booed non-stop one Saturday night at Glasgow Empire. I thought that, being a Scot, she'd be interested. She probably was, for the first hour. But let's face it, after that it would be difficult for anyone's interest not to flag. I must say, she was incredibly patient.

Shouting one's mouth off to strangers is a dangerous practice, particularly if you're in the armed services – and I'm not just thinking about national security and the Official Secrets Act.

Take the example of the unfortunate corporal who'd managed to get on the wrong side of his CO – for once not Gunner Howerd, I'm pleased to say. This bloke had had hell from his superior and a deep resentment had built up inside him. In fact not to put too fine a point on it, he loathed his guts. One evening he was letting off steam at a party talking to a very pretty girl, when his commanding officer came in.

'That's the miserable old devil I've been telling you about,' he said, looking in the CO's direction. He's the meanest bastard I've ever come across.'

'Do you know who I am?' asked the girl sweetly. 'I happen to be that "miserable old devil's" daughter.'

'Do you know who I am?' asked the corporal hastily swallowing his drink.

'No,' said the girl coldly.

'Thank God for that,' said the corporal, and disappeared into the throng.

Handle with care

When Ted Pertwee started to make it big in the building trade, he was, like a lot of builders, not slow to splash his money around. He bought a new car. He bought his wife an expensive fur coat and decked her out in large, gaudy, and very expensive pieces of jewellery. Mrs Pertwee wore her newly-acquired gems on the slightest pretext and when she was 'going out somewhere posh' she used to dress herself up like the Queen of Sheba.

One evening when she was being entertained by the head of a business consortium that was in the process of buying a factory that her husband had just built, she began shouting her mouth off to her host's wife. The woman had been unwise enough to admire the dazzling array of precious stones that Ethel Pertwee was wearing. She said that the insurance premiums must be a worry but Ethel shrugged this aside with the observation that she let the tax man take care of that.

Then she started on a blow-by-blow account describing each piece and how she acquired it and when she'd last worn it. She even went into details about the way she looked after the contents of her jewellery-box.

'I clean my sapphires with fresh goat's milk, my diamonds with ammonia, my rubies with lighter fuel and my emeralds with five-star brandy. What do you use?' she asked pointedly.

'Oh I never bother,' said the host's wife. 'When mine get dirty, I just throw them away.'

Aide-memoire

I knew a journalist who suffered from 'face dyslexia' — at least that's what he called it when he passed me in the street without even registering who I was only a day or two after writing an article about me. If it hadn't been for his wife pointing me out to him, he might have missed me completely, which would have been an awful shame.

It's awful to forget a name when you recognize the face and when the face obviously knows who you are. You either spend half the time listening to what the face is saying and the other half trying to remember where the hell you met before. Or else you just have to admit defeat and make some pathetic apology for your 'appalling memory'.

One smooth sales representative when confronted with young women on his rounds whose names he had forgotten, used the perfect line to get over his embarrassment and come out on top.

'I didn't bother to remember your name, when we met,' he would remark with total self-assurance, 'because I felt certain that your looks and your accomplishments would soon force you to change it.' Most of the young ladies who fell for that ploy seemed to be flattered rather than affronted.

I reckon this idea could be taken a stage further and used with distinguished-looking, middle-aged men, the ones who usually hold the purse-strings and whose names you have no business forgetting. All you'd have to do with them is to apologise, but say that you'd thought that they'd been made a life-peer, or given a knighthood by now.

At least that's better than being caught in the same frightfully embarrassing position as Sir Thomas Beecham who noticed a distinguished-looking lady in the foyer of his hotel one evening but could not for the life of him put a name to her familiar face. They chatted awhile then, suddenly remembering that she had a brother, and in the hope of identifying her, Beecham asked her how he was and whether he was still in the same job. 'Oh yes, he is very well,' she replied, 'and still King.'

It must be something to do with being a conductor, for Sir Malcolm Sargent apparently had a similar problem with names one day when a member of Scandinavian royalty was present at one of his concerts. During the interval he entered the royal box with his leading soloist. 'Your Majesty, may I introduce Sergio Poliakoff?', he said proudly. 'Sergio – the King of Norway.' The monarch shifted uncomfortably and murmured, 'Er-Sweden'. Trump that, Sargent!

EVEN MORE RULES OF HOWERD
(try and cope! Every so often you might come across a gem)

---

1) Never admit to being in the wrong. If you put your foot in it, don't try and go back on what you've said or done. By all means try and turn your *faux pas* to your advantage, but if you can't, go out in a blaze of glory. Back-tracking prevents you from doing even that.

2) When you're getting your own back always go for the most obvious line of attack. Don't try to be too subtle if you can answer in kind.

3) When in doubt, flatter. It doesn't cost much and the pay-off can be remarkable.

4) In every social crisis stay in control of events. That way you can direct them to the best outcome from your own point of view.

5) If you can't think of any way out of a jam, stay quiet. Other people may not notice it and if they do the onus is on them to start throwing the muck.

6

For Services Rendered

(preferably without payment)

In the good old days of self-sufficiency it was every man for himself, and winner takes all. But today, if you've got a problem which you can't solve on your own, you're bound to have to get in someone else to help you, and as soon as you do not only is the inefficiency factor doubled, but the costs too. With plumbers running at around £8 an hour, garages pushing £10 an hour and solicitors charging you £25* for wiping your feet on the door-mat, it's amazing that the whole fabric of our life hasn't been torn up in outraged panic.

There was a time, not so long ago, when people seemed genuinely pleased to be of service – I can remember being like that myself. Not that they grovelled pathetically for work – at least only once in a while. They actually seemed to enjoy giving value for money (but then there was a time when the trains were punctual and when the bus companies paid their way).

Of course, right at the other end of the scale come the people who force their attentions on us free of charge and who turn out to be just as much of a pain in the neck as the ones who couldn't give a damn whether they fixed a dripping tap or not.

*By the time this tome is published the rates will have doubled, you mark my words.

Since it's virtually impossible to get satisfactory service from anyone these days, from the coalman to your MP, unless you make a confounded nuisance of yourself, it seems to me that the only answer is to get as much pleasure as you can out of seeking revenge, like the good people that follow.

Things weren't always so selfish and cut-throat. There was a time when a spirit of national comradeship accounted for a lot – like with my concert parties in the army during the war. God, did people help out then!

During one of these series of shows I got an act together with a couple of other blokes in which we dressed up as ATS girls and sang a little ditty, of my own composition. The act was a huge success, so much so that we'd sneak off to concerts without official passes. Once, we clean forgot our three vital costumes. What did we do? We borrowed them. We hunted the streets for three ATS girls that fitted our various sizes: one midget; one six-footer, thin as a bean-pole (me); and the third, just as tall but stouter. You may not believe it, but we struck

gold. Goodness knows how, but we managed to find the three girls we needed and conned them into coming to the concert. In the interval we asked them: 'Would you mind if we borrowed your uniforms?' And, bless their hearts, they didn't fail us. They sat in their khaki bloomers, shivering in the toilets, while we did our bit on stage in the uniforms. Though I like to think we made it worth their while later on.

Satisfactory progress

I don't know about you, but hospitals give me the willies – no, not hospitals themselves, they're just buildings. But they're so full of weird goings-on that half the time one is completely in the dark. It's terrible what the imagination will do when you're lying flat on your back day in day

out, with nothing to do and with a thermometer being regularly shoved into any convenient orifice.

George Stokes from Leighton Buzzard was in just that position after he'd been admitted to the local hospital for a minor operation. His problem was that he didn't really feel any different after the operation, and whenever he asked one of the doctors, or one of the nurses, how he was progressing, they always used evasive terms like 'fair' or 'satisfactory' which didn't tell him anything.

In the end George couldn't stand the suspense any longer, so he asked for the bedside telephone provided by the Friends of the Hospital. Then he put through a call to the hospital switchboard and had his line connected to the sister's office on his ward.

'I'm ringing to enquire about Mr George Stokes,' he said, 'I'm his father-in-law. How's he coming along? Did the operation go all right? Were there any complications?'

The nurse who answered the phone gave George much fuller answers than he'd been able to get earlier and before she asked any more questions he thanked her for her help and put down the receiver, greatly relieved by what he'd been told.

Face lift

When it comes to getting one's own back actors ought to have a head start. Many of them are very quick-witted. But I'm impressed by the way people with no theatrical training at all carry off marvellous pieces of ad-libbing, which I'd have to be plastered to attempt. Take this bloke for example.

Gerald Churt of Paddock Wood, Kent, popped into a snack-bar in nearby Tunbridge Wells one busy lunch-time and paid through the nose for a piece of dried-up bread and a lump of very old cheddar that was being excused by the management as a ploughman's lunch. He left feeling both ripped off and mighty peckish.

He went back to the snack-bar three weeks later, not to eat this time, but to measure the place. A surveyor by profession, he had the equipment and the vocabulary to be convincing when he was discussing building work. He chose the start of the lunchtime rush and then set to work.

Without speaking to anyone he started measuring the snack-bar from wall to wall and from end to end, making notes in a pad and muttering things like: 'Main partition wall to right of entrance with access to strong room and vaults.' He'd also brought along Colin, a friend from work, to hold the other end of the tape, to whom Gerald made comments like: 'We'll have the lorry back up to this big window, so make sure they get the glass out first thing. Then they can drop the premix straight through without having to get a licence for using the pavement. O.K.?'

Then moving to the side of the snack-bar and getting in the way of the queue that was forming at the counter, he said: 'Right. Here's where they'll put the cashier desks. We'll need a conduit for the security system when those boys move in. Can you make sure Len knows that before he puts the new floor down?'

By now the owner of the snack-bar had come over to Gerald to ask what he was doing.

'Don't ask questions now,' he told him brusquely, 'I'm in a hurry. We've got three more jobs to do this afternoon.'

'What the hell do you mean "Don't ask questions"', said the proprietor. 'I run this place. What the blazes do you think you're doing in here?'

'I'm just working from the plans,' explained Gerald as he reeled in his tape and made his way through the queue to the back of the snack bar, behind the counter.

'What plans?' asked the proprietor, his voice rising an octave.

'The ones for the alterations, of course,' Gerald told him as if stating the obvious.

'What alterations?'

'How should I know?' replied Gerald, writing quickly in his pad. 'I'm only the surveyor working from the plans, but by the looks of it they'll be putting the Crown Jewels in here. Let's measure up for the steel doors, Colin.'

'Now, just a minute, what about my lease?' yelled the proprietor.

'Don't ask me,' said Gerald, 'you'll have to take that up with the landlord. We've just been told to come down and measure this place up. It's taken too long as it is,' he said, indicating to Colin that they should go. 'See that Len gets rid of that window tidily. We don't want glass all over the pavement like last time. And don't let him get that premix too early. The last lot nearly went solid before he was ready to use it.'

And with that they left the snack-bar and its proprietor fighting back through his customers to the telephone to give his landlord a piece of his mind.

Ah, sweet revenge!

Trade-names

There's only one thing worse than listening to a DIY bore droning on about house maintenance – that's paying the builder hand over fist for a job which you know damned well he's made a packet on. But if you're as useless and impractical as I am, what the hell do you do? Live in a tent, I suppose.

When Mr and Mrs Dave Lawrence moved into their house in Blackburn they got a quote from a local builder for the alterations they wanted. The builder didn't take long to weigh up the job and gave them a price of £1,500, which sounded too good to miss. It was.

Before long the builder was knocking on the kitchen door when Dave was out at work saying that he needed 'a couple of hundred quid in cash for some more slates'. Then he started making noises about the floor in the loft which ought to be replaced, and before too long Dave realized that they'd end up spending well over twice what he'd originally told them. Dave certainly didn't have that kind of money, so he blew the whistle on the extra work and concentrated on getting done all that was needed.

After he told the builder this, the work began to tail off. Days passed without any sign of the boss or his mates and when they did show up, it was only to ask for a bit more money 'in advance'. By the time Dave had paid over £750, he was getting fed up with paying out for so little activity. So he wrote a letter to the builder saying that he wouldn't pay any more money until the job was finished. In the meantime he'd discovered that materials for which he'd supposedly paid cost price had in fact been sold to him at over three times the correct price. Dave Lawrence didn't like being cheated so he set about getting his own back.

After writing to the builder once more to ask him to get on with the work, Dave started sending a letter a week to the local Chamber of Commerce, asking them to help him. Then he took the builder's sign, which suspiciously had never been erected, and stuck this inside his car against one of the rear windows. Dave was a travelling salesman in the Blackburn area and he made sure that he parked his car in the most conspicuous places when he was out on business. The sign claimed that the builder undertook 'Demolition, Renovations, Roofing, Drainage and General Building work.' Before putting the sign in the car he had added a touch of his own – the words 'If you're Lucky' written in big red letters.

After three weeks of 'advertising' and three letters to the Chamber of Commerce, the builder reappeared, finished the job in two days, charged Dave £1,300 (after being reminded about the £200 for the slates) and left with his sign muttering oaths and curses about 'legal action'.

Dave Lawrence is still waiting for the summons.

Now you see it, now you don't

When I was thirteen I was a Sunday School instructor, which might sound hard to believe, but in fact I was very popular – mainly because I deviated somewhat from the script. Robin Hood featured in my classes considerably more than St Paul, but none of the kids minded. In spite of this success, I never felt inspired to take up teaching – there seemed to be quite enough unsuitable people doing it.

The visiting instructor at one technical college I heard of, a Mr Unman, didn't seem very happy with his lot. He complained about the timetable. He complained about the room in which he was supposed to give his lectures, saying that the ceiling was likely to fall in at any minute. And most of all he complained about the students whom he though were lazy and foolish.

Alan Jowett, one of those unfortunate enough to come under Mr Unman's wing, wasn't lazy or foolish, but he didn't have a very high opinion of Mr Unman's powers as a lecturer. Half-way through one term Unman sprang a surprise test on his students to check on their progress. The results were predictably disappointing and as a punishment he told the whole group to attend an extra lecture at the end of the course, on the first day of what was to be the vacation. This meant special arrangements with the college caretaker, who was none too fond of Mr Unman as it was, because of his constant complaints about the lecture-room ceiling.

The night that the official term ended, Alan and a group of other rebellious students sneaked into the lecture room after dark. While one of them painted a large jagged hole in the ceiling, the others covered the floor with broken plaster that they'd picked out of a nearby skip. Then they turned up the following morning for their extra lecture to see how Unman would react. He took one look at the hole and the débris on the floor and dashed out of the room to get the caretaker, full of righteous indignation. It took him a good ten minutes to

86

find the poor man and haul him along to the lecture room. During that time Alan and the others had swept up all the plaster into a dustbin bag and had washed the black paint from the ceiling. Because it was still wet and because they had spread vaseline onto the ceiling before painting it, there were no traces left when Unman stormed into the room with the caretaker. His final lecture didn't have the impact that he hoped it might.

Call out

Plumber Wally Joyce, from Bootle, used to go through hell every winter. As soon as there was a thaw after a severe frost he started getting calls in the middle of the night from people whose pipes had burst. He'd have to go out at all hours and in all weathers. It paid well, mind you, but it took its toll on his health. Where most people got colds Wally went down with 'flu and he usually spent the time he wasn't working lying miserably ill in bed.

It was his chest which always got it worst and there were times when he coughed so much at night that he'd have to call the doctor. After the first few visits the doctor had given up coming out in the middle of the night for the same old complaint. He used to repeat the same treatment down the phone and then go back to sleep. However, the treatment didn't often work, so poor old Wally would spend a wretched night until his wife could pop down to the chemist in the morning.

Then one night Wally's phone rang at half-past one. It was the doctor, up to his ankles in water, yelling at Wally down the phone to come over and help him out.

'Sounds like the usual problem to me, doctor,' said Wally. 'Drop a couple of aspirin down the plug-hole every four hours and give me a ring during working hours if that doesn't help!'

He had to find another doctor, but he slept well that night!

One for the road

Isn't it irritating how cars always pack up just when you need them most? I've been stranded on the M4 before now, on the way to do a show in Bath. Did anyone stop? Did they hell! Not that I can blame them, after all it was dark, on a busy road – and the flashing lights must have made me look like something out of a horror movie. In the end it was the local Chief Constable who did the honours, bless him. If he hadn't I could still be standing there. On another occasion three of us broke down on the M1 in the small hours of the morning and it was only my accompanist's white dress that attracted the eye of a lorry-driver and got us a lift to London. The driver even got me to sign an account of what happened so he could show his mates. Cars! I wish we still had horses.

When her own Mini packed up in Lincoln the day she went into town to do her week's shopping, Mrs Rosemary Macpherson of Bardney was forced to take a taxi home. The taxi driver filled the boot of his Ford Granada with

her shopping and charged Mrs Macpherson twenty pounds for a journey that was less than ten miles.

When they reached her home, he told her that he had to charge extra for every individual piece of luggage, and Mrs Macpherson had several baskets, not to mention an assortment of plastic carrier bags. After protesting till she was blue in the face at this daylight robbery, Mrs Macpherson paid the man and began to collect her bits and pieces. On top of one of these was a bag of potatoes. Standing behind the taxi she noticed that the driver couldn't see her as he was getting comfortable in his seat before driving off. So, grabbing the largest potato she could see, she pushed it into the taxi's exhaust pipe until it was stuck fast. The taxi drove off seconds later, but Mrs Macpherson knew that it wouldn't get very far. A warm glow of satisfaction came over her as she pictured the taxi-driver's face when he discovered that it wasn't his fuel gauge that was wrong.

Typing errors

I once tried to type – once. So I can well imagine how disappointed the chairman's secretary was when the new typewriter arrived and she found that, far from speeding up their work, it made life in the busy office even more difficult. She'd had previous dealings with the suppliers and knew that in the ordinary run of things it would be weeks before the typewriter was looked at. The following letter got her the attention she needed without delay:

Dxar Sir,

Wx hxrxby wish to acknowlxdgx the rxcxipt of your shipmxnt of onx of your xxtra-spxcially quixt typxwritxrs.

Howxvxr, upon opxning thx shipmxnt wx found that for thx timx bxing wx shall bx sxvxrxly handicappxd. In gxnxral, thx typxwritxr is in pxrfxct condition xxcxpt for onx small dxtail.

Through somx xrror of assxmbly thxrx sxxms to bx

rathxr an xmbarrassing omission – thxrx is no
lxttxr on thx machinx for 'x', thx fifth lxttxr of thx
alphabxt.

Will you plxasx bx so kind xithxr to sxnd us
anothxr machinx or havx this onx sxrvicxd as soon
as possiblx.

Sincxrxly,

Xlaine Xvans, Sxcrxtary to thx chairman.

A lesson in grammar

You may well wonder who am I to sound off about
English grammar. But let me assure you that any little
solecisms (that's one word I know for a start – if not the
meaning) that may have passed my ruby lips have always
been part of the act. Furthermore I've never had the
audacity to set myself up as another Fowler or Partridge
(and I know they're nothing to do with shooting, either).

I'm prepared to admit that there are some people who
are perfectly entitled to put the rest of us right when we
happen to wrong. But they can be very tiresome. There
was an agent I came across who fell into this category.
Script-writing was none of his concern really, but he took
a perverse delight in correcting what he saw as little slips
in grammar. It gave him a sense of superiority and lost
him what few friends he had.

Anyhow those who were unlucky enough to make his
acquaintance made it as short as possible. He used to sit
in style in a fairly large office, full of secretaries dashing
about looking busy, making what he thought were
important phone calls and dictating pedantic letters.
That's until one morning his phone rang and the voice on
the other end said:

'I'm very sorry to disturb you, Mr ********. My
name's Wilkes, Leonard Wilkes. I'm a writer, working on
the script for ************ **** **** and I've come up
against a problem. It's been puzzling me for years, in fact,
and no one's ever been able to give me a satisfactory

answer. It's a grammatical problem, you see ... and I've been told that you might be able to help me.'

'I'll do what I can,' said the pedant, basking in recommended glory.

'Well, it concerns the use of "is" and "are". I want to use the word "souls" with the verb "to be" but should it be "is souls" or "are souls"?'

'That's really very elementary,' came the reply, 'It should be "are souls" – I'm surprised it's been troubling you.'

'Sorry, can you repeat that, ... I'm in a phone box and the traffic's making a frightful din outside.'

'Are souls', said the advisor, raising his voice.

'What?'

'Are souls.'

'I'm sorry, you'll have to shout, there's a lorry parked alongside now.'

'Are souls. Are souls! Are souls!!' the man screamed down the phone and he'd probably have carried on like that if he hadn't suddenly noticed that the office had ground to a standstill, the girls nearest him blushing with embarrassment.

Service with a smile

The number of times I've been on the point of giving wide-boy salesmen a knuckle sandwich is nobody's business. These jokers reckon they've got carte blanche to mess me about all in the name of fun – and all in the name of getting me to cough up more of the ready. Thank God I'm not the only one.

Mark Nicholson of Taplow, Bucks regretted buying an expensive foreign car as soon as he started having to pay the garage bills. The franchise garage he had to take the car to for any service was fifteen miles away and apart from the spares costing the earth, the garage manager was the type of greasy, smooth-talking, milk-you-for-all-your-worth con man that Mark couldn't stand.

After owning the car for three years Mark finally decided that he'd get rid of it and buy an English car, which a friendly garage down the road could service for a third of the cost. So on his last visit to the garage with his foreign model he planned to show the manager what he thought of him now that he wasn't going to be at his mercy any more.

As usual the manager came out to see Mark when he arrived to pick up the car and write out another huge cheque. The bloke was quick to point out the extra little services that he'd provided (and charged for outrageously). And, as usual, he said to Mark as he was getting into the driver's seat: 'Can I fill you up with petrol?'

'No thank you,' Mark told him.

'Would you like the windscreen washed?'

'No thank you?'

'Perhaps we'd better check the air in the tyres now that the car's outside.'

'I'm sure they'll be all right.'

'How about a quick wax polish. We can get you done in ten minutes with the new gear?'

'It looks as if it's going to rain, it'll have to wait.'

'Well, is there anything else I can do for you?'

Mark played his trump.

'Yes, there is,' Mark said. 'Could you just stick out your tongue so that I can seal this letter?'

Forty-love again!

RULES OF HOWERD

1) When you want to get your own back or you want to make the maximum amount of fuss always choose the time of least convenience to your enemy. If it's a business you're getting at, direct your attack for the beginning or the end of the working day. Better still, if you're gunning for an individual try to pester him or

her at home.

2) Always give criticism where it is due. It's only because we're too mealy-mouthed as a nation that things have got so bad.

3) If you're complaining about someone else's laziness or inefficiency do all you can to make the offender work to put things right, even if you are completely to blame. Then when the poor devil's finished the work, apologize, since you've suddenly remembered that it was all your fault!

7

Touching the Law

(without being familiar)

Let's come clean, it's usually a fair cop, isn't it? That's if you're talking about minor infringements of the law, the sort you and I get hauled in front of the beak for. The more serious the crime, however, the easier it seems to be to get off the hook, but that's democracy for you.

Wriggling your way out of any legal trap is a tricky business, unless you and the magistrate belong to the same golf-club. I don't play golf as it happens, so, almost by definition, I'm a guilty party. I just keep my nose clean and hope for the best.

The real catch in the whole legal business is that honesty sometimes isn't the right policy. Now I'm not saying we should all let rip and forget about the law entirely – that's anarchy. No, what I'm driving at is that when you're in a jam, you've got to cook up some sort of convincing diversion to spring on the forces of law, either while you make up your mind what you're going to say, or better still, while you make a run for it.

Though if it's any consolation, the officers of the law, for all their virtues, aren't always infallible. If I were you I'd never take chapter and verse for an answer. It never does any harm to give the law the once-over yourself. There may be a loophole somewhere – after all, what else are lawyers for?

Sheer, blind, unashamed bluffing can work wonders, too, when you're hard up. I remember one night during the war when a couple of mates and I were out to do a concert in the town. We'd scrambled out through a hole in a hedge since we couldn't get official passes. There was supposed to be a war on, but we reckoned it would manage without us – and we were right. It managed for another five years. Anyhow we got stopped by the MPs in Southend High Street, of all places. As luck would have it, we all had our proper kit, rifles, gas-masks, the whole ruddy lot. So at least we didn't look as if we'd just sneaked out of camp on artistic business. Still, one of my mates, a sergeant in the Pay Corps, had a brainwave and, pointing at me, said sternly: 'Prisoner and escort. We're taking him to the glasshouse in Colchester' – where we'd all have been heading, minus our stripes, if they'd arrested us instead of waving us on.

We all thought it was a great bluff at the time, until a thought struck me. Why did nobody query our story? What if Francis had been a spy, eh?

Bribery and corruption

To my way of thinking, the idea of the small claims courts is an excellent one. It relieves the main courts of much of the time-wasting, minor cases that they had to deal with in the past and it gives both parties a chance to thrash out their differences face to face. It has an added advantage for those who are prepared to bend the rules a little, as this example shows.

Two motorists collided at a T-junction in Tooting. One was driving out of a one-way street, the other was slowing down peering at the new 'No Entry' sign before speeding up and trying to find his way into the street through another road. Each of them was blowed if he was going to admit responsibility for the accident and they finally chose to settle their case in the small claims court where an adjudicator could hear what they each had to say, before making up his mind who was guilty.

The motorist who thought that he stood the least chance of winning the case was the one who had been driving along the main road and had slowed down to look at the sign. His case needed a bit of help, he decided. So he made a few discreet enquiries and managed to prise out of a court official the name of his adjudicator. His next move was to buy a dozen bottles of expensive claret and send these to the adjudicator's home.

Suicidal, you might say, except that he sent the claret in the other driver's name!

All in the line of duty

Let's face it, without booze most of us would be sunk. A couple of jars and all your inhibitions start to melt away. Two more and you're more confident than ever. Two more after that you'll take on anyone. And two more later, you do. Naturally you don't exactly help your cause if you drink and drive, but just occasionally a bit of Dutch courage can get you out of a scrape...

Ernie Milligan from Garstang, Lancashire, usually went on a bender with the other lads from the works at Christmas-time. Their gaffer was pretty reasonable about letting them off early on Christmas Eve and most of them didn't bother to get out of their overalls, they just went round to the local as they were and got smashed.

One year Ernie had been out on a job and had driven straight to the pub with his tools. He'd missed the first couple of rounds and had to make up for lost time. His only problem was that in catching up with the others he quickly lost count of how many pints he'd had. By the time the landlord turfed them into the street Ernie was well on the way.

It was obvious that he was the least fit to drive the van back to the works, so one of the others volunteered to do it for him while a couple of the lads helped him home. The fresh air and some fish and chips made Ernie feel stronger again, and he told his mates that he could make it back himself. So they left him with his tool-box and went home themselves. Ernie had been on the optimistic side, though, and a couple of streets later he tripped on the pavement and the next thing he knew, he was spread-eagled on the grill in the gutter with his tools lying all round him.

Lying down felt more comfortable than standing up, so he decided to stay put. It was while he was lying there that a policeman walked over and asked if he was all right in a way that implied that he was damned certain that Ernie was anything but all right.

'Yes, fine', said Ernie, with great aplomb, looking up and reaching for his tools. 'Fine, except for this darned mains connection. I've been lying here trying to get my hand down to reach it, but I can't get it far enough down because of these bars. The old girl inside will go spare if I don't fix it this afternoon, but like I told her, it's not my fault if they put the blessed thing in so that you can't reach it. Here, you haven't got a truncheon on you, have you? That might just shift the blighter.'

'By all means,' said the policeman, now sounding far more respectful. 'Just drop it down carefully, won't you?'

Ernie carefully looped the leather thong round his fingers and poked the truncheon down through the grill. He made one or two swipes at the 'mains connection' and then made contact with a pipe sticking out of the wall. 'Ah, that's the bugger!' he exclaimed triumphantly. 'One more for luck,' and he gave the pipe another clout with the truncheon.

'Thanks ever so much,' he said to the policeman as he handed it back. 'Now I can get on.'

'Always glad to be of help,' came the reply and the policeman walked off down the street. Ernie had a quick look to see that the coast was clear, picked up his tools and then lurched off home for a cup of tea. A damned close-run thing.

The case of the missing earl

Not so long after a well-known police investigation went cold, a drinking mate of mine told me this strange tale over a glass one evening.

Tony Saunders, an acquaintance of his, had just moved into a new flat in Hendon. It was a tip, and Tony had to spend every evening of his first week trying to get it straight. He rarely got to bed before three in the morning, and his work began to slip. He nodded off over his drawing-board on Wednesday afternoon and by Thursday evening he was all in. He pressed on, though, and with a burst of enthusiasm finished painting his kitchen at dawn on Friday morning. When he woke up six hours later he had a bright new kitchen, but he'd probably lost his job.

The head of the plans department was a stickler for timing and discipline. There wasn't any point in trying to telephone through an excuse, Tony knew. He'd have to bite the bullet and face him man to man. He had an idea how to handle him.

'The truth is, Mr Smallweed, that my mind's not been on my work this week... you might have noticed,' Tony began.

'It did come to my attention,' said Smallweed.

'It sounds absurd, but I realized on Monday that I was being watched,' said Tony, pressing on.

'Being watched?'

'Yes. There's been someone outside the flat every night this week, either in a car or on foot. Well, this morning they got me.'

'Who got you, Saunders?'

'Scotland Yard, sir. I was leaving at 8.20 as I usually do when this car drew up beside me and three men jumped out and grabbed me. One of them said, "Would you mind answering a few questions, my lord?" And another said, "I must warn you, Lord Lucan, that anything you say will be taken down and may be used in evidence against you." Of course I protested that I wasn't

Lord Lucan, but they didn't seem to believe me.'

'But Saunders, you don't look anything like Lord Lucan,' said Smallweed, with stunning perception.

'That's just it, sir. They're working on a tip-off that he's had a face change. Someone's seen me pottering about late at night in my new flat and reckoned I was behaving suspiciously. So they hauled me in and asked me questions about where I'd been and what I'd been up to. I wanted to phone you, but they wouldn't let me speak to anyone. They said that they'd been on my tail for months and weren't going to have things loused up now. Anyway, it didn't take me long to prove who I was, at least it didn't take them long to see that they'd got the wrong man. But before they let me go they said that it had all been off the record, because they didn't want word getting about that they were still picking up suspects. They seem convinced that he's still in London.'

'And how do you propose to avoid this confusion in the future?' asked Smallweed. 'We can't have our employees being whisked away every time they set foot outside the door, can we?'

'That's easy, sir. They've given me official clearance now that they've checked me out. I expect someone will ring later on this afternoon to see that I've turned up here. But they warned me that they wouldn't disclose who they were. Shall I go and get on now, I've wasted enough of your time today?'

Tony put the call through to Smallweed that afternoon from the coin box in the gents. He stuffed a hanky into the phone and affected a thick Scottish accent. When Smallweed called him Commissioner and said that Mr Saunders had arrived, he knew he was all right. But he did the rest of his decorating at the weekends.

Counter-argument

A bank robber in America, some years ago, decided on an unusual method of demanding money. He wrote out his instructions on a piece of paper.

'This is a stick-up and I've got a gun', the cashier read as the paper was pushed under the grille.

Then came another piece of paper. 'Put all your money in a paper bag,' it said.

The cashier played what must have been one of the coolest trumps of all time. He wrote on the bottom, 'I don't have a paper bag', and pushed the piece of paper back.

Unnerved, the robber took to his heels.

It pays to be accurate

No one could accuse me of being a pedant when it comes to the use of language, as you will have gathered. But I do at least pride myself on knowing when some types of languages are acceptable and when they aren't.

Not so with the American car-dealer who took Louis Glick of Cincinnati for a ride. Louis had sold his car to the dealer for what the dealer claimed was a fair price. But he felt cheated when a friend who had an identical model sold his a few days later for a good five hundred bucks more than he'd been paid. So, being an innocent soul, he went back to the dealer and asked if he could have a bit more. The dealer told him where to go.

Then, to make matters worse, only a couple of days later Louis passed the dealer's yard again and saw his old car advertised for $1,795, which was only just short of double what he'd been paid. Sure, it had been resprayed and the tyres looked different, but Louis saw red all the same. He also saw that the dealer had advertised it in an unusual way. No doubt to attract the right buyer, he'd plastered the windscreen with the sign 'For Sale – 1,795 bananas'. (Bananas, incidentally, used to be a slang word for dollars. For all I know it still is.)

Either anger or inspiration suddenly fired Louis with determination to see this business through to the end. He went to the nearest fruit store and bought fifty bananas, which he then offered to the car dealer as a down-payment on his old car. For the second time the dealer told him what he could do with himself.

Louis wasn't beaten. He got the local cop to witness the sign on the car and then took legal action against the car-dealer for false advertising. The dealer lost and Louis agreed on a settlement. He paid over the balance of the bananas and in return the dealer gave him the keys of his car once more.

Why is it that I can never come up with minor coups like that?

Road test

You do see some funny sights on the road. When I was out East I once saw a dead buffalo going for a ride in a rickshaw – God only knows where it was off to.

A woman in Bracknell, Berkshire, once telephoned the Thames Valley Police in a state of absolute panic to report that she had just seen a car passing by with a body lying in the boot. The woman described the colour of the car and its general shape. She remembered that it had four doors and two radio aerials at the back. An alert went out to all patrol cars in the area and within a quarter of an hour of the alarm being raised a panda car in Bracknell pulled the offending car in to the side of the road. The woman had been absolutely right. There, sticking out of the boot, were two legs.

The policeman driving the panda car radioed his HQ and reported that he'd got the car and was about to make an arrest. His HQ told him not to take any unnecessary risks and the copper approached the car with caution. He was level with the driver's window when a voice from the rear of the car said, 'What've you stopped for, Bert? I was just getting near it then.'

The policeman looked down at Bert and then stared at the boot of the car. The lid lifted and out got a man dressed in overalls. He and Bert worked for a garage and they'd taken the car out on the road to try and isolate a rattling at the rear when it was driving along.

Ambulance self-service

An Irish motorist named Rooney was stopped by a policeman who suspected that the car he was driving wasn't fit to be on the road. His suspicions were well-founded.

Mr Rooney's seventeen-year-old Mini, which had only cost him £6 from a passer-by in the first place, wasn't just uninsured, it was an absolute death-trap. The brakes didn't work; all the tyres were bald; the steering wandered all over the road; the spare tyre was flat; there was no rear-view mirror and the car was coated with mud. The only saving grace was that the gearbox was so far gone that only the first gear worked and that kept the speed down to walking pace.

Before arresting him, the policeman was curious as to why Rooney was driving the old banger – he'd probably have been better off asking how. Rooney was unrepentant. He had broken his leg trying to jack it up to repair it, he explained, and as he hadn't any other way of getting to hospital he thought it was better to break the law than go without medical treatment.

Freshly baked

Speaking of excuses, get a load of this one...

Seeing a Bedford van roaring past them at fifty-four miles an hour, when it was in a thirty-mile-an-hour zone, the two Newhaven policemen gave chase. The driver of the van, Mr Irving Schold, pulled to the side of the road immediately and was very contrite when asked why he was breaking the speed limit at half-past-six in the morning. Ruling out the possibility that he was drunk, the police were suspicious that he might have been on his way home from the scene of an as yet undiscovered

crime.

But Mr Schold was able to put their mind at rest. He explained that he had no idea of the speed at which he was travelling because the consignment of bread, straight from the ovens, which he was carrying in the back, had steamed up his speedometer to such an extent that he wasn't able to read it accurately. He assured the policemen that he would take greater care in future and offered them a couple of freshly-baked loaves in case they were peckish. His kind offer was refused, but he went on his way a free man.

Saved by the toe

One of the great reliefs of my life is that in all the scrapes I've got into with motor cars (usually with them breaking down, I hasten to add) I've never been nabbed for drunken driving. More to the point, I've never given any reason to be hauled over to the side and asked to blow into the little plastic bag.

The same can't be said of John Forster, from Sacriston, Co. Durham. After a car owned by him had inadvertently forced a police car to the side of the road, John was carted off to the nick and asked to give a blood sample.

In spite of his state, he had the presence of mind to tell the doctor that he could certainly take a blood sample – from his big toe. Now I didn't know this, which shows my innocence in such matters, but apparently the usual places from which blood samples are taken are the thumb, the arm, or the ears. Big toes don't get a look-in and the police doctor refused to take a sample from the suspect's big pinkie. This proved to be a fatal error of judgement.

The case duly came to court and the police doctor told the jury and the bench that Mr Forster had refused to give a blood sample. However, the razor-sharp defending solicitor pointed out that there was nothing in the law that prevented a blood sample from being taken from any part of the body. What's more, the prosecution's allegation that taking a sample from the toe would lead to a risk of infection would surely apply to the rest of the body, too? The magistrates listened to this learned discussion about John's anatomy with interest, but when it came to passing judgement, they weren't in any doubt. John couldn't be guilty, they said, because he had complied with the law as far as it went. So he was acquitted.

Whipped

Here's an example of a brilliant trump, given backing by the full weight of the law. A few years ago the *Manchester Evening News* reported a case in America in which Mr John Cherry, editor of the *Seattle Times*, on being told that his defence against a libel charge was hopeless, agreed that the plaintiff, Mrs Diana Line, instead of receiving damages should be allowed to pelt him with custard pies.

He duly turned up on the steps of the newspaper's building, dressed in a bathing costume and a face mask. For some reason no custard pies could be located in Seattle so Mrs Line and her two young sons threw giant chocolate creams topped with raspberry dip at poor Mr Cherry (an appropriate name, in the circumstances) until he was covered in the stuff.

The lawyer for Mrs Line said: 'I have had clients who got more money but none who got more satisfaction.'

Glazed look

Derek Robertson was pressured into buying double glazing but because the recession had stopped all over-time he found he could not afford it. He then dreamed up the perfect plan to get money to pay for his new double glazing. It was a trump he was sure couldn't fail.

He decided to snatch the wages at the company where he had been a 'model and trusted employee' for 20 years. He bought a toy gun and made himself a Klu Klux Klan mask. He planned to slip away from his workbench, grab £11,200 in the wages room downstairs, do a quick change and return to his work as though nothing had happened.

But things went wrong. As he was waiting to ambush the men delivering the wages he was called back to his bench by loudspeaker. By the time he returned he had missed the delivery. The door was locked and he could not get in.

'He decided there was no going back and picking up a fire extinguisher he hurled it through the window of the wages office,' said Mr G. Richardson, prosecuting at the Old Bailey. 'He frightened the staff with the imitation gun and ordered them to put the cash into a bag he had with him. But there was too much money and he had to ask them to get him another bag.'

Robertson then fled to the lavatories with the loot to remove his disguise but found his way blocked by other staff. Still in the mask he ran into the street straight into the firm's security man.

The security man decided, 'This huge robber is too big for me', and called for the help of the firm's largest employee – none other than Derek Robertson.

As he was yelling: 'Get Derek,' his prisoner said tartly: 'I am Derek, you fool.'

RULES OF HOWERD

1) When you're searching for an excuse that's going to cut ice with the law either go for the most outlandish or the most hypocritical. Nothing in between will do.

2) If you do find a way out of any prosecution, keep it up your sleeve. You might need to use it again in the future and bragging about your success will only get your loophole sewn up.

3) If you get into prolonged dealings with the law keep your head. The correspondence may seem farcical. But don't let on that you're taking it as a huge joke. The bloke you are corresponding with probably thinks it's important and he won't thank you for ridiculing him.

4) With the price of car parks going up through the roof, seriously consider where you park. It might work out cheaper to park on the yellow lines if you're only going to get a fine every so often.

5) Always pay your fixed penalties. Going to court never works out cheaper.

8

Community Relations

(et tu, Brute)

When I was younger and a church-goer, being more saintly, I was imbued with the idea of loving my neighbour. Then I got a bit older, left home and moved into my own flat and acquired neighbours. Being some-what less saintly by this time, I sometimes found it difficult to obey this commandment (or any of the others come to that). It's all very well being told to love our neighbours as ourselves, but when they don't show too much love in return, you tend to reach a crisis in your faith, not to put too fine a point on it.

What makes it worse is that the word 'neighbours' doesn't just include the folk next door. It's usually the whole street and the people behind, too. I sometimes think the only really good neighbourly relations are the ones where you keep out of each other's way. Mind you, neighbours can be a problem (don't worry, they're probably saying exactly the same about you) so what happens when your nerve does snap and you feel like banging a six-inch nail through the bleeder's loose garage door at two in the morning because it's keeping you awake? Well, I'm no hero, so I'd probably let it go at that if I could, but if you do do anything, it's safest to settle your score without being found out – apart from anything else, there's less need to move house if you do.

All right, you might think I'm being feeble, but I'll tell you, there have been times when I've been moved to act, and it's always ended in disaster (and I'm not referring to my stage career, thank you very much).

There was an occasion in 1963 when I was doing a very tiring show, *A Funny Thing Happened* ... in fact, so I needed my beauty sleep like nothing else. I was blissfully away in the land of Nod at seven-thirty one morning when an awful racket started right outside my window. Some geezer with a pneumatic drill was carving up the mews in which I lived. Now I don't like drills at the best of times and, feeling as I was, I went spare. I leapt out of bed, blundered to the window, went to fling it open to give him a piece of my mind, and, in so doing, smashed the glass and cut my wrist. Of course I had to go to hospital to get it stitched up and, to cut a long story short, the press got hold of the news and thought I'd tried to do away with myself, though God only knows why since I had just made a West End comeback that would have seemed impossible two years before.

Anyhow, I've stopped rowing with neighbours since then. I suggest you do, too – if they'll let you.

Ambush

In 1978 a 20-year-old youth sprang upon 74-year-old Mrs Ethel West while she was walking through Chichester Cathedral. The result should have been a foregone conclusion but Mrs West turned the tables in a way which the mugger could never have imagined. Having taken a course in judo when younger she first grabbed his wrist, at which he cried out, 'Oh God! Oh no! Stop!' then, emboldened, she put him in an arm lock at which the youth yelled out, 'Oh no, Oh Christ'. His superior strength finally carried the day and he escaped but, as Mrs West emphasized. 'If I hadn't been carrying my shopping I'd really have put him on his back.'

A case of mistaken identity

In spite of what my adoring public, and some of my less adoring critics, may say to the contrary, Francis Alick Howerd is not filthy-minded and vulgar. That the art of innuendo has not passed me by, I won't deny, but, as they say, it takes one to know one. Seaside humour of the good old belly-laugh type is fine in my book, but I've always drawn the line at filth.

Mind you, you see a lot of it in the theatre, or should I say in the auditorium. I remember whan I was doing a revue with Winifred Atwell, called *Pardon My French*, the stage was littered with topless girls. This was back in 1953, Coronation Year (not that that's got any bearing on what follows), when, far from prancing around, the girls

were under strict orders to stand stock-still, like statues. But this didn't prevent some of the raincoat crowd from coming and leering at the company that Winifred and I were keeping on stage.

The girls themselves were marvellous. They'd developed a splendid resistance to such perverts, and I reckon they enjoyed mocking the situation. One of these splendid young ladies had finished rehearsing early one day and had left the theatre to walk home. She had popped into a telephone box to ring a friend when this dirty old man approached the door. As she pushed it open to leave the pervert whipped open his mac and said: 'What do you think of that, then?'

She played the greatest trump card of all.

'It looks like a prick to me,' she said, pushing past him, 'only a bit smaller.'

Childish curiosity

Frequently it's not the neighbours themselves that are the problem. It's their blessed kids or pets that are the real headache.

Frank Selsey lived in a large Victorian house that had been divided into flats, about five minutes from the river in Twickenham. Generally speaking he got on very well with his neighbours, though being a bachelor he found it difficult to put up with their children at times. The family that lived immediately beneath him, the Thomases, had a litle boy called Derek. Derek was an only child and his parents doted on him. But he was the last thing in precociousness and he could never turn down the chance to see how anything worked. He'd already buggered up his father's stereo in the pursuit of this knowledge.

On Derek's fifth birthday his parents unwisely presented him with a toy drum. Young Derek spent most of his waking hours wandering through the flat beating an uneven rhythm on his new toy. Frank got on well with

Derek's parents and he didn't want to upset them by complaining about the noise. The only way he was going to shut Derek up, therefore, was by somehow nobbling the wretched drum. He thought about stealing it but gave up that idea because it was never out of Derek's sight. Then he hit on the perfect solution.

On his way back from work a week after Derek's birthday, Frank popped into a nearby modelling shop and bought a cheap set of child's carving tools. None of these were particularly sharp but they all looked suitable for Frank's purpose.

Going down to the Thomases' flat he knocked at the door and it was answered by the late birthday boy himself. 'Happy birthday, Derek,' said Frank with his hands over his eyes, 'I know I'm terribly late with my present, but here's something to say sorry. My, is that the drum you got from your Mum and Dad? I had one like that when I was your age. Does yours have a picture of a soldier on the inside of the drum-skin?'

'I don't know,' said Derek eagerly opening Frank's present. It didn't take him long to find out that there wasn't a soldier inside his drum.

Meals on wheels

Miss Nancy Scott-Martin didn't have a lot of time for people who enjoyed the countryside from their driving-seats. She'd spent all of her fifty-two years in the saddle and had probably ridden as far as she'd ever travelled by car.

The old trout lived near Lyndhurst in the New Forest, where she ran a riding school and battled to keep the countryside intact for those who lived there. She had twenty acres of paddocks and exercise fields which were festooned with signs warning trespassers not to enter. And she made it virtually impossible for anyone to get in even if they wanted to. The only ones she couldn't keep away were picnickers who parked on the verge and fed her horses on sandwich spread and synthetic chocolate biscuits.

Miss Scott-Martin had given up trying to stop these people, she just kept her horses away from the lane at Bank Holidays and during the peak holiday periods. But one day, while she was mucking out the stables, an irate man in a shirt decorated with what looked like musical instruments stormed down her drive and started laying into her about her horses and their eating habits. It wasn't that they disliked his sandwiches. What had got this motorist hot under the collar was that they'd started tucking into his car — an orange sports car. The man in the gay shirt (her words, not mine) said that he was going to sue the old bag for all she was worth for what the horses had done. So Miss Scott-Martin downed tools and went with him to the scene of the crime.

As soon as she saw the car sitting behind the hedge in her field she knew she was safe. Despite the sign warning him to keep out, the man had driven under the barrier, which would have stopped most cars, but not his, which was very low. And it was obvious from his lady friend who was dressed in what Miss Scott-Martin described as 'gym-shorts and singlet', that he hadn't just been looking for somewhere for a quiet picnic.

'The horses thought your car was a carrot', said the owner of the field, hands on hip, standing her ground. 'I wouldn't be surprised if they haven't damaged their insides with the paint and loosened a few teeth on the bodywork. There'll be vet's bills to pay, you know, as well as the charge of trespassing. I've got your number so don't think you'll get away with this. Now be off with you and take your wife with you!'

Embarrassed and discomforted, they fled. The man in the shirt cursed and swore as he bumped and bounced towards the gap in the hedge. But he cursed and swore even more when, after skidding to get into the lane, the car suddenly lurched forward and left the silencer with its matching chrome tubes sitting in the feeding trough that had been lying hidden in the grass.

Kept in the family

During my earlier years in showbusiness, because I considered life had been good to me in many ways, I felt very strongly that I ought to show my gratitude by helping out with charitable causes – for instance, making a certain number of appearances every year without payment. Because I also felt that it was rather immoral to gain publicity out of other people's suffering I often insisted on there being no publicity. All this was very worthy – and very stupid! One day I was visiting a handicapped people's school and as usual insisted that there should be no press. I explained my motives with apt humility, only to receive a tirade from the principal who said, 'Don't you realize that they would love their pictures in the paper and *we* need the publicity.' I learnt.

But thinking of charities, so to speak, when the Ablethorpe parish council decided to build a village hall they organized one of those elaborate campaigns to raise funds. There was a village fête for the first time in fifteen years. There were dances and village parties, and a vigorous door-to-door collection was organized by the local lady of the manor.

While making personal calls to all the people in the village whom she thought ought to cough up for the hall she visited a man who was reputed to have made a million from various undisclosed business deals involving property in the neighbourhood.

'I'm certain that you won't begrudge a generous donation to such a worthy cause when others far less able to spare their money have given so generously already. Besides as a man who has made his living in the area you will want to feel that you are part of the community by contributing to a village venture like this.' Her ladyship didn't beat about the bush when it came to screwing money out of wealthy men from the lower orders.

She was in for a bit of a shock in this case. The millionaire didn't deny that he was rich. But he told her ladyship that most people seemed to forget that he had three wives that all demanded money from him, not to mention eight children, all at private schools. In addition he had to look after both his elderly parents and a grandmother, not to mention relatives living overseas who were always after money, too.

Her ladyship was taken aback and apologized: 'I'm very sorry, I didn't realize that you were giving away all that money.'

'I'm not,' said the millionaire, 'so you can't expect me to give money to total strangers when I don't even give it to my own family, can you?'

Artistic merit

Mr Noel Huggett of Staxton, Yorkshire, had been an amateur artist ever since he was given a box of paints for his tenth birthday, and what he may have lacked in skill he made up for in determination. Mr Huggett had devoted all his spare time to his art and his house was littered with his masterpieces.

Sadly there were not many other people who shared Mr Huggett's enthusiasm for his own work. He'd tried offering his paintings as prizes in local raffles and fêtes, but every time they had been rejected by the organizers. His greatest indignity came when he tried to exhibit his best paintings in a show dedicated to local artists and found that none of them was accepted, even though paintings which he thought were far worse were given pride of place, and sold for very high prices.

Mr Huggett felt so furious with the organizers that he decided to take drastic action. As an artist himself he wouldn't have dared damage any of the exhibits, but he was determined to get the people running the exhibition into a rare old flap. On the night before the exhibition was due to close he left a crowbar and several empty picture frames on the steps of the exhibition hall. A policeman found them a few minutes later at 2.50 am and the exhibition organizers were summoned from their beds to check if any paintings had been stolen.

Door-step evangelists

It's curious how the crusaders for our souls always seem to knock at the door when we're at home and we haven't got a cast-iron reason for not discussing the finer points of St Paul's conversion with them over the threshold. Experience suggests that there's only one way to deal with people like this, always assuming that you don't want to get involved with their theological debates. You've got to be blunt and absolutely committed in your dismissal. Any sign of weakness on your part, any mumbled apology about 'not having the time just now, but perhaps if you'd like to come back when...' is an open invitation to a course in fundamental brainwashing. At the risk of sounding curt, even offensive, you've got to lay it on the line as soon as you open the door.

Forget about George Bernard Shaw's famous remark when a couple of people came knocking at his door, said they were Jehovah's witnesses, and Shaw answered, 'Good, I'm Jehovah, how are we doing?' No, a more modern but equally evasive line goes something like this: 'Sorry, you're too late. We had the Unification Church round last week and they scooped the pool. We're all Moonies, man. Fancy joining up yourself?'

There was an inspired lady in Hastings who had planned her response and when she heard the knock at the door, greeted her saviours dressed in a bath-towel and beating a saucepan with a plastic fish-slice singing 'Hari Krishna, Hari Krishna'. Her visitors fled when she proffered them a smouldering piece of baking paper stuffed with artificial grass from the hamster's cage.

The other way out is to sum up the status of your visitor and then go one better. If you reckon that he or she's C of E, say you're Baptist. If Baptist, say you're Seventh Day Adventist, and if it looks as if you're face to face with the hard core put on your best Irish accent and announce blithely that you've become a Catholic again.

The idea of all these ruses is that they give you a couple of precious seconds in which to slam the door while the Bible-basher on the other side is getting over the surprise of coming up against something more ardent than a few murmurs of discontent about the Alternative Prayer book.

Taken short

The only time I've ever really suffered severe internal disorders was when I got the galloping trots during a frantic concert party of the eastern Med. Like a fool I'd had an ice-cream in Port Said.

Mind you, you don't need to be incontinent, or have Delhi belly, to feel those sudden calls of nature when there isn't a convenience for miles around. If you do have to flee into the undergrowth, or, worse still, have no choice but to turn your back on the passing traffic, there's every reason to be well prepared. Follow the example of William Ferry of Plaistow, who was caught relieving himself on the public highway.

There was no point in denying the accusation since he'd been nabbed red-handed, so to speak. But Mr Ferry was able to play his trump card; his defence was ready. He indicated a notice attached to a nearby tree, which bore the word *Gentlemen*, and claimed that he wasn't committing an offence because he had hung up the notice before setting about his business. Apparently he always carried the sign with him to deal with just such an emergency.

There was also a true story of a famous old comedian, who was a friend of mine – and who told me how he was once caught in dire straights in a crowded compartment in a train with no corridor – if you know what I mean.

Two things came to his aid – a long, dark tunnel, and a bowler hat. It's true, I swear it.

Neither a borrower nor a lender be

The only time I ever cadged seriously off other people was when I used to pop down to see my old landlord, Ben Warris, to 'borrow' a cup of sugar – though I usually left with a loaf and coffee as well. Even when I was on my uppers I tried not to sponge off my mates.

When Ernest Kidworth was building his garage he found that he needed to drill a series of large holes into the structure before he could complete the construction of the frame. He had his own drill which he could use. What he didn't have was a bit large enough for the bolts he had to use.

Next door lived Harvey Ingram, a do-it-yourself fanatic. Ernest knew that he had a masonary bit that was large enough for his job and he went round to Harvey to ask if he could borrow it. The miserable sod said 'No'. He didn't lend his tools to anyone, he said, and that was that.

Several months after Ernest had finished his garage, having had to go out and buy a masonry bit to drill ten holes, he was walking his dog past Harvey's house one Saturday afternoon and saw that the front door was open. There wasn't any sign of Harvey or his wife in the garden and after tapping on the door, Ernest realized that they must have popped out, forgetting to shut the door. He nipped inside, saw a pad of paper and a pencil by the telephone and scribbled an almost unreadable note followed by an unreadable signature. Then he tore this off the pad and left it by the phone.

Later in the afternoon he got a frantic phone call from Harvey saying they'd found a note but couldn't work out who it was from or what had been taken. A few days later when Ernest bumped into Harvey again he still hadn't found out the answer to his question, but he told Ernest that he'd checked through all his tools and couldn't find anything missing. His wife had spent a couple of evenings going through the kitchen doing the same thing, he said with an air of desperation. For the only word that *was* legible on Ernest's note had been the word 'borrowed'.

Answer-phone

Parties. Now you're talking my language. I may not be the world's greatest cook, but, though I say it myself, I have given some fabulous fish-and-chip parties in my time – very easy-going affairs with a friend I was working with. I remember Richard Burton, who had a passion for nuts, sitting on my floor many times, like a squirrel, surrounded by empty shells. Now everyone expects showbiz parties to be loud and boozy. All right, some of mine were, but with my double-glazing and getting friends to leave quietly, very few of my neighbours ever got ratty. All it takes is a little consideration.

Louis Halling and his wife Cathy of Hockley Heath, Warwickshire, enjoyed having a good time, too. They liked entertaining and they often had a crowd of friends round on a Friday night for a few drinks and a bite to eat after the pubs had shut. The party usually carried on until the small hours of the morning.

Louis was always very careful about disturbing the neighbours. Their front-room was fitted with double-glazing which cut down most of the noise and he always got his mates to leave their cars in the pub car park so that they wouldn't wake the people nearby when they left.

This arrangement worked fine – with one exception, George and Renée Roper, who lived two doors away. They couldn't really hear any noise from the Hallings but they hated to think of anyone having a good time when they weren't. So they regularly made a fuss about the noise. This didn't amount to much really, until one day Louis got a visit from a policeman saying they'd had a complaint and it was his duty to call round and ask Louis to be a bit more careful in future. Louis asked how many people had complained and the policeman admitted that it had only been one couple. Louis knew it was the Ropers without having to ask.

The following Friday he and Cathy held court as usual and, in the small hours of the morning, deep into huge beakers of Spanish wine, Louis began telling all his friends what a miserable old bugger George Roper was. One of his friends suggested they really *did* spoil George's sleep.

The friend, whose name was Alf, found George's number in the phone book and dialled it. George was fast asleep so it took him a few minutes to answer the phone.

'Is Sid there?' asked Alf, when George picked up the receiver.

'Sid who?' asked a sleepy George.

'Sid Weaving,' said Alf.

'You've got the wrong number,' George told him.

'Sorry,' said Alf and put down the phone.

A few more cups of wine later, one of the other men dialled George's number. He went through the same process of asking for Sid Weaving and apologizing for the wrong number before he put the phone down. This was kept up until George had well and truly lost his temper. Then the final call was made by Louis's brother Dan.

'George?' he asked.

'Yes, this is George. What do you want at this time of night.'

'This is Sid Weaving, George. Any messages for me?'

RULES OF HOWERD

1) Never do anything that will jeopardize your standing with the neighbours you're *not* getting at.

2) Whenever possible cast the net of doubt as wide as you can.

3) Never refuse to contribute to community activities or funds *without* having a cast-iron reason for not doing so. It doesn't matter whether you invent this on the spur of the moment, but you must have a definite, hard-hitting response to requests of this sort that will knock any prying questions smartly on the head.

4) Be bloody-minded to anyone who is bloody-minded to you. Mark Twain tells the story of the man who agreed to let Twain borrow a book on the condition that Twain read it in the man's library. When the man later asked Twain if he could borrow his mowing machine Twain agreed, providing the man used it on Twain's lawn.

9

Fun and Games

(well, games anyway)

Surely it's not too much to ask that the one time when you ought to be able to get away from the usual scrapes and bumps of life is when you're enjoying what's laughingly called your leisure time. But, as everyone knows, you run just as much chance of coming a cropper when you're trying to have a good time as you do when you're sweating blood over your desk, or being hounded by the fuzz.

It isn't easy, either, to summon up your fighting instincts just when you've taken them off for a bit of a rest. And then there's the added problem that the sort of disasters you run into when you're having a good time usually involve other people – notably your family, or your friends.

There's usually only two choices. If you take the wrong one, you end up with egg all over your face. What lies the other way? Triumph and totally unexpected success. Want proof? Learn from the works of Howerd.

In the bad old days, before the government loosened their grip on our spending, we weren't allowed to spend more than £25 abroad. Sounds laughable today, doesn't it, considering you couldn't buy lunch in many places for that price, but it was true. You probably remember. Well, I'd gone off to the South of France with my sister and a couple of friends for a week in search of the sun. At the end of the week, we heard that Josephine Baker was appearing at a nearby casino, so we took ourselves off to listen to her over a gin and tonic each, which set us back £11 – in the days when £11 was £11. The bill left us speechless and as good as penniless. I think we had £1 between us, which wasn't even enough to get us to Nice airport.

None of us knew what to do. But something inside me said 'Go on, try your luck' and without really realizing what I was doing, I went back into the casino, got an entry card and used all the cash I had to buy some chips. Then I went to the nearest roulette table and stuck the money down on a few numbers.

I won exactly £11 on that spin of the wheel (no, I didn't go on to win £1,100, I was a sensible boy in those days; besides I'd never gambled before). I just cashed in the chips and went out to rejoin Betty and the others. It was only when I saw the look of horror on their faces that it dawned on me what I'd just done. But the gamble had paid off, literally. It's a bloody shame a few of the later ones didn't as well.

Chopin's socks

Every performing artist, from the man with jumping fleas to the prima ballerina, lives in apprehension of the critic who has a hangover or a pain in his back, or just a good old-fashioned dislike for that particular type of act. God knows, I've taken enough stick from critics in my time. But how it smarted at the time.

There are those who can take it philosophically, and those who make damn sure the critic suffers as a result. I tend to fall into the first group. The great Russian pianist, the late Vladimir de Pachmann, was a champion of the other lot.

Pachmann was a marvellous showman as well as a superb pianist (he's reckoned by many to have been the

finest interpreter of Chopin. I prefer Rubinstein myself, but I'm very fond of Chopin anyway.) Apparently Pachmann would come on to a stage to play and appear to find the piano stool too low. Then he'd whisper to someone in the wings and get them to fetch a great thick book for him to sit on. But this he'd find too high. So he'd stand up again, tear out one page, and try it once more. A smile of satisfaction would spread across his face and he'd start his concert with the audience in his palm already.

But critics were a different matter. Pachmann loathed them, and there was one, who fancied himself as a Chopin buff, whom he hated above all others. This chap used to write long, erudite articles about Chopin which Pachmann regarded as a load of bull, and after a couple of scathing reviews of his performances, he decided to teach the wise guy a lesson.

At his next concert the maestro walked on stage proudly holding a pair of socks. He went down to the footlights and announced that these were the very socks that George Sand had knitted for Chopin. After a suitable pause to let the full effect of this piece of history sink in, he returned to his piano and ceremonially draped them over the instrument to inspire his playing.

The next day, as he had hoped, the critic arrived at Pachmann's door and asked if he could see the socks. Pachmann invited him in. As soon as the man had the socks in his hands, he began fondling and kissing them with blind adoration. However, his nose can't have been up to much. Pachmann had been wearing them continually for the past fortnight, as he made a point of telling everyone after the critic had paid his homage.

Distant relatives

Remember Groucho Marx's immortal line, 'I wouldn't dream of belonging to any club that would have me as a member'? Well, here's a little trump that should put all club bores on their guard.

When Paul Double of Twyford, Berkshire, proposed a friend of his for membership of a local sporting club he didn't expect the application to be rejected out of hand by the secretary. But it was. Paul received a very curt letter in reply saying that there were no vacancies for new members of his friend's line of business and there would not be any in the foreseeable future. Paul was more than a little annoyed.

In answer to the club secretary he wrote a letter of his own, but not with his own name at the bottom. He addressed the letter from Keighley, in Yorkshire, where his daughter was a teacher, and signed it Alfred. Alfred was a distant cousin of the club secretary invented by Paul. He lived alone with his elderly mother, Auntie Ciss, in a run-down terraced house. Alfred's first letter filled the club secretary in on 'any news of the family which you might have missed recently'. It described in gory detail Auntie's latest operation for her varicose veins and described Alfred's increasing attraction to the Salvation Army. When the letter was finished Paul addressed it to the club secretary and put it into an envelope with a note to his daughter asking her to post it for him. Then he sent it off to her home in Skipton, just up the road from Keighley.

Over the next weeks Alfred wrote to his distant cousin regularly and in each of his letters he described his old mother's ailing health. Finally he wrote saying that she was being sent to a specialist in London because their own doctor could no longer do anything for her. Without wishing to appear too pushy, he made it perfectly clear that they wanted to come and visit the club secretary while they were down south – 'and maybe we can come and have a cuppa in that club that you belong to?'

The visit never took place, but Paul noticed that the club secretary kept an uneasy eye on the main entrance for a fortnight after he sent that final letter. He thought later that he should have written to say that Auntie Ciss had passed away. But when he remembered the way that his friend had been treated he decided he'd rather leave the club secretary with that nagging anxiety in his mind – was he going mad, or was there really some dreadful branch of the family in West Yorkshire that was about to descend on him – and please God not during the Medal Championship...

Exit notice

Naturally most of my experience of clubs has come from the stage – and that can be a pretty hairy experience at times. I've played midnight spots in some clubs where the audience has been drinking solidly for six hours. Sometimes it's just a sea of heads, at others you can't hear yourself think for the hecklers and the abuse you get. But at least you don't usually get slung out of the club as a performer.

Under normal circumstances Andy Burton would have left the club without question. If he'd known that he was supposed to be wearing a tie he'd have brought one with him. Seeing that it was a topless club, though, he felt a bit hard done by when he was told he'd have to go. He didn't make a fuss that time. He reckoned he'd get his own back later.

Andy worked for a small printing company in Barnes. During his spare time he did a little printing of his own. The management only charged him for the materials and a little for the use of the machine and he often earned a bit on the side doing letter-headings or business cards for friends. This time Andy ran off a few cards of his own – smart, expensive-looking cards with a simple message: 'The management would be obliged if you would leave the club. Please go quietly.'

He went back to the topless club several times after that first disagreement with the bouncers and each time he took his cards. He used to pick his targets carefully and then slip a card onto their table while they were dancing or at the bar. Then he'd retire to the shadows and watch the punch-up that followed.

Command performance
(a fête almost worse than death)

Desmond Macdonald didn't have a lot of time for the pompous, county set, but he did believe in helping charities. So when a member of the local nobility announced that she was going to hold a charity fête and was going to call upon local artists and craftsmen to assist her, Desmond Macdonald thought that he might be on her list of subjects. He was. When his invitation came, he didn't throw it in the basket, he wrote back saying that he would be willing to help if he could. In reply he was sent a printed card telling him to present himself at the lady's mansion early on the morning of the fête.

When he arrived he was shown into her ladyship's drawing-room where she was holding court. 'I'm not going to waste time telling you what to do,' she announced when she'd checked Desmond's name against her list and ticked him off as 'artist'. 'You're going to paint a picture for this fête this afternoon. There are going to be a lot of significant people there, so I want a painting which is going to sell well. It is for charity, remember?' Then she dismissed Desmond and called in the next artisan, a wood-carver.

Outside Desmond was presented with watercolours, an easel and paper. He asked the butler who exactly was coming to the fête and the butler told him that two hundred invitations had been sent out to promiment people in the neighbourhood. Desmond said that he thought it was going to be open to the public and the butler told him that he didn't think that was quite what her ladyship had in mind.

Finding a quiet corner of the grounds, away from the bunting and marquees, Desmond set to work. No one saw him tearing sheet after sheet from the pad and no one checked up on his progress. After a couple of hours he'd finished his work and leaving the easel and other materials under the tree where he'd been working, Desmond walked nonchalantly down the drive to the large wrought-iron gates beside the little stone-built lodge. The lodge-keeper and his wife were busy up at the big house and they didn't see Desmond decorating the entrance to the house with the signs he had been painting: 'Open Day'; 'Bring all the family'; 'Free Parking'; 'Fun Fair and Amusements'; 'Non-stop Bingo'; 'Dogs Welcome'; 'Pick Your Own Flowers and Veg'; 'Swimming Pool and Boating Lake'.

The first car was turning into the drive as Desmond caught the bus home. The subsequent report in the local paper spoke of 'some confusion' at the start of the charity fête which was eventually sorted out with the aid of the police.

Chef's speciality

Luckily for my bank account at times, I've never been one

for the rich food and fine wines. I'll happily tuck into a Chateaubriand and a tasty Burgundy with the next man, providing he's paying, but on my own I'm just as happy with simpler fare. In fact one of the things I dislike about eating in posh restaurants are the smart alecks who reckon they're one up on Egon Ronay or the Galloping Gourmet. From the looks I've seen waiters give them, I'm not alone either.

There was one clot I heard about who used to go overboard about tripe. He went on and on about one particular way of serving tripe which was second to none, but the local restaurant where he usually ate didn't serve this particular dish. I don't know why he bothered to eat there at all, because all he did was complain about the food and send little messages to the kitchen to tell the chef how he could improve his bearnaise sauce.

This went on for several months until one day the owner of the restaurant had an idea while in his Turkish bath. Forsaking his usual massage he hurried back to the kitchen and explained his scheme to the chef. Together they got together the ingredients for the favoured dish, which meant dashing around delicatessens trying to find obscure herbs just before closing time. But they managed it, and when the gourmet sauntered in at his usual hour the owner greeted him with a surprise. He said he'd taken the man's advice and given the chef the sack. The new chef was a wizard, he explained, and as a special tribute to the gourmet's superior judgement, he'd had the chef prepare the dish of tripe he'd always raved about.

The man was delighted and after a light *hors d'oeuvres*, the tripe was brought in, covered with the sauce that had been carefully prepared. The aroma was exquisite. The gourmet sniffed it lovingly and then set to with his knife and fork. Pausing only to tell the owner that he'd done the right thing by getting rid of the man who didn't know the first thing about tripe, he cleaned his plate and sat back with a look of self-righteous triumph. The look changed when he called the bill, for in

place of the tripe, was a bill for a flat sponge from the Turkish bath, which, parboiled and served with the sauce, he had just adoringly consumed.

First Strike

Getting your retaliation in first is a maxim which applies to many sports. I suppose it's like a pre-emptive strike in war: it has the advantage of complete surprise. But probably no one has taken it to quite the extreme that Roberto Rivelino did on a football field in Brazil. One second after the kick-off in a match between Corinthians and Rio Preto, Rivelino scored with a fierce left-foot drive from the halfway line. The ball whizzed past the ear of the Rio Preto goalkeeper, Isadore Irandhir, while he was still on his knees in the goalmouth finishing his pre-match prayers. That trump, however, was quickly trumped in its turn when the goalkeeper's brother, incensed by the fraternal humiliation, ran onto the field, drew his revolver, and fired shots into the ball.

If all that seems somewhat unnecessary, pity poor Ralph Walton who, in 1946, was knocked out in 10½ seconds in a fight in America. No sooner had the bell rung for the start of the fight than his opponent bounded across the ring and hit him as he was still adjusting his gum shield in his corner. Needless to say this shortest fight on record contains 10 seconds while Ralph Walton was counted out.

Name dropping

I've done enough pantomimes up and down the country to have learnt that Christmas is never a good time of the year to try to get last-minute tickets at the theatre. Seats that have been empty throughout the rest of the year suddenly get booked up for weeks in advance and surprise treats for the kids just aren't possible. Such was the fate of Gordon Hughes of Alton, Hampshire. He made the disastrous mistake of offering to take his kids to *Jack and the Beanstalk* before checking that he could actually get the tickets. When Gordon rang the box-office and was told that there weren't any spare seats he was up a gum tree.

Gordon knew that his wife, Lindsay, would hit the roof if he fouled up this of all treats, because he'd had months in which to get it organized. Therefore he kept quiet and tried the theatre again asking if there was any way in which he could get four tickets. The woman who answered told him that he might be lucky if some tickets were returned but he'd have to be there on the night to buy them just before the curtain went up. It was a glimmer of hope, but it was still horribly hit-and-miss as far as Gordon was concerned.

He was confiding his misery to a friend over a pint one evening when salvation appeared at the mention of house seats.

'What are house seats?' asked Gordon.

'Every theatre keeps them back for each performance,' said his friend, Derek, 'just in case they've made a cock-up with the bookings. Then, if everything's all right, they sell them just before the play starts.'

'That's fine,' said Gordon, 'but what do I do if there's a waiting list for tickets. Some of these blighters have been pestering for over a week. They'd be bound to get the tickets first.'

'You'll just have to pull rank,' said Derek. It set Gordon thinking who to impersonate.

Providing he paid for the tickets in cash, no one would be able to check his name, so within reason he could be whoever he liked. He decided he'd have to go for someone that no one in the theatre had ever seen, so that ruled out the royal family, the entire government, most leading stars and every top sportsman Gordon could think of. At the same time his man had to have some clout with the theatre, otherwise he couldn't get in at all. He tried to work out what theatres respected most apart from stars and reps from the booze trade. Famous directors seemed a possibility but that could lead him into hot water if he found himself invited back-stage afterwards, or asked to write a short piece on the show. No, his man had to be powerful but anonymous. Gordon thought of all the powerful and anonymous people he most feared and realized that they were all connected with money. That was it. He'd have to pretend that he was tied up with the theatre's finances.

The Arts Council sprang to mind as the obvious choice, but after a quick thumb through *The Stage* he decided to go for CORT, the Council for Regional Theatre. The chances were that the staff wouldn't know the names of any of the CORT bigwigs. Even if they did, the sight of Gordon talking in a dinner-jacket to one of the men would probably make it easier to convince the other people waiting for tickets that he was a VIP.

Once he'd got his plan worked out, Gordon waited for the day of the show. At lunchtime he phoned the box-office and asked if there were any spare tickets. He was told that the show was sold out. 'In that case could you make a note of my name in case any are returned this evening,' he asked, and the woman on the other end duly made a note of the new CORT chairman.

The family got to the theatre forty-five minutes before the pantomime was due to start, and Gordon left them in the bar while he went to the box-office. He asked if any tickets had been returned yet and was told that some had been, though these had been given to people higher on the waiting list than Gordon's name. He went back to the bar, bought the kids another Coke and gave his wife another large vodka and tonic. He had a whisky himself, to settle his nerves, and then went back to the box-office to try again.

The weather had turned nasty and a few more people had phoned up to cancel their seats, but there were still several names waiting above Gordon's. There were now twenty-five minutes to go before curtain up and Gordon's hands were turning sweaty. 'I wonder if I could have a quick word with the manager?' he whispered through the box-office grill.

'I'm afraid that the manager's not in this evening, sir,' the lady on the other side told him, 'but I can get the house-manager if you like.'

'Thank you,' said Gordon and waited nervously beside the door.

A few minutes later the house-manager came up to him and asked what was the matter. 'I don't like to be pushy,' Gordon began, 'but I'm staying down here with my in-laws and the kids are mad keen to see the show. I tried to get four seats this morning, but you know what it's like and from the way things are going, it doesn't look as if we're going to get in on the returns either. The point is CORT likes to take an active interest in theatres like this and I would appreciate it if we could squeeze in somewhere. I don't suppose the house seats are still free by any chance?'

'I'll just go and check, sir', said the house-manager and he disappeared into the box-office.

Gordon saw him whispering to the lady selling the tickets and he saw her look in his direction and pick up the list of names of those waiting to buy tickets. He'd managed to avoid saying who he was pretending to be, hoping that the phone call and his appearance at the box-office would do the trick. It did. Seconds later the house manager appeared with four tickets for the stalls stamped *Complimentary*.

Gordon felt a bit awkward about this since he'd always intended to pay for the seats, but the man refused point-blank. Then in the nick of time he saw a sign advertising a fund-raising appeal for the theatre. Making sure that the house-manager could see, he went over and donated the ticket money he had in his pocket.

He had just enough time to buy himself another drink, refill his wife's glass, apologize to the family for having had to dash back to the car to get the tickets which he'd left under his seat, and buy the kids a box of chocolates before the bell went to summon them into the auditorium. Gordon hadn't enjoyed a pantomime so much for ages. To my mind, he showed brilliant *élan* – a true trump, if ever there was one.

Fill-in

Cinema attendances for *Gone with the Wind* now exceed the 200,000,000 mark, and some people are reported to have seen it again and again. But there is always a new audience for it, and one day in 1980 when the projector broke down in a cinema in Coventry, the manager and

the ice-cream sales girl leaped onto the stage and themselves acted out the famous parting between Clark Gable
and Vivien Leigh. Their presence of mind certainly saved

the day. As the manager said afterwards, 'I wouldn't say we gave an Oscar-winning performance, but at least the customers went home happy knowing how it ended.'

RULES OF HOWERD

1) When alcohol features in your strategy make full use of it. If your opponents can be driven to show the worst of themselves through having drunk too much the results are always much more rewarding.

2) If the reason for your particular disaster has prevented you from enjoying yourself or achieving what you set out to do, the best and most satisfying way of getting your own back is to deprive the others of their enjoyment.

3) Success in sport is not always the most effective way of being 'good' at it. Frequently it is just as important to give the impression of being good. Gamesmanship has won as many games as proficiency.

10

On the Go

(or trumps up and away)

Travelling these days is getting to be more and more of an ordeal and travelling disasters are too numerous to catalogue. Just sticking to one means of transport lays you open to an incalculable number of possible calamities. So when you take into account what could happen by a simple combination of British Rail work-to-rules, motorway repairs, channel ferry strikes and air-traffic controllers' go-slows, it takes guts even to set foot outside the door at all.

Sometimes the cause of our fury is the organization we're paying through the nose to take us from A to B. Sometimes it's other travellers who make one see red. And not infrequently it's one's own means of transport, usually the car, which plays up, and throws everything haywire.

But as long as we choose to remain an island, we're going to have to get used to travel, which means that we'd better get used to handling travel problems before they send us screaming round the bend.

I've played Korea during the war. I've played Borneo, travelling round in a helicopter, which one cheerful Charlie told me was one of the sort which were dropping 'like flies' out there, because of the heat; and I've done concert tours of the Mediterranean with a tummy as loose as some of the stages I had to appear on. But for sheer, nerve-racking fear, nothing matched my tour of Cyprus.

I went out there in 1974 to lend a little moral support to our chaps who were caught in the punch-up between the Greeks and the Turks. Now my own wartime training was some thirty years before and in the intervening years Francis had become softened by the years of peace. To put it bluntly, I was terrified when we landed at Nicosia airport, which just to confuse things was uneasily divided between the opposing armies, with a narrow corridor running between them. Needless to say we had to drive down this.

I hit the deck as soon as we climbed on board the truck. I'm nobody's hero when it comes to getting caught in the cross-fire. But the driver moved so damned slowly that I was convinced we were going to be shot at at any moment. I wasn't cheered either by the major escorting us, who pointed out that at one stage we had to drive perilously close to the Turkish lines.

I'd like to be able to say that I stood up and greeted our NATO brothers as we passed, but that would be

telling a big fib. In fact I was crouching down. The person who was really responsible for getting us through without a scratch was the gorgeous blonde who was travelling in the party with me, the lovely Julie Ege.

As we neared the Turkish lines you could see these chaps lower their guns and stare at this stunning creature driving serenely past like something from a Greek legend. They were so mesmerized I don't think they'd have fired back even if the Greeks had launched an attack at that precise moment. Thank God we had the Ege.

Finger tight

Like a lot of commuters Mr Raymond Mutch from Burgess Hill, West Sussex didn't take kindly to the way he was treated by Southern Region. His particular complaint concerned the station staff that shut the doors before the trains pulled out. On several occasions Mr Mutch had got his brolley jammed in the door and once he nearly lost a leg as he sprinted inside a carriage and the door slammed shut behind him. He'd complained to Area Managers and as many people in British Rail uniforms as he could find, but he never got any satisfactory apologies and he kept on having close shaves with slamming doors. One employee even suggested that he might try getting to the station a little earlier. Mr Mutch walked away from him in disgust.

Eventually he decided that attack was going to be his only means of defence. So he went to the nearest Scout Shop and bought one of those imitation fingers on which they practise injuries and dressings. As an ex-Scout, I can vouch for how nasty these things look. He spent the evening removing the artificial gore and making the finger look as normal as possible. Then for good measure he slipped a fairground ring, which one of the kids had won, over the knuckle and popped the finger in his pocket.

He didn't have an opportunity to use it for a couple of

days, but when he noticed one of the prime door-slamming culprits making his way down the train just as it was about to pull out, Mr Mutch deliberately pushed his door open a little wider and waited for it to slam shut. He'd opened the window specially too, and as the train rolled out past the railwayman he gave the door a mighty shove and it closed with a sickening crunch (a carrot that Mr Mutch was holding ready by the catch). At the same time Mr Mutch let out a cry of agony and dropped the finger onto the platform.

Looking back down the platform he saw the railwayman turn, look at the finger and drop like a sack of potatoes. Mr Mutch never saw him slam a door again.

No smoking

Brian Larch from Newton Abbot found himself on the slow train to London with nothing to read and nothing to look at out of the windows because of the driving rain.

Absent-mindedly he took out his packet of cigarettes, put one in his mouth and lit it.

'Can't you see that you're in a No Smoking compartment, young man?' snapped a tweedy woman sitting opposite him.

'I'm very sorry,' said the offender, stubbing out his king-size on the floor, 'It's just a habit,' he explained.

'Habits can be cured,' persisted the old dragon, 'My husband hasn't put a cigarette in his mouth for years.'

'Really?' said Brian, 'I've never tried putting mine anywhere else.'

Tickets Please

Two Englishmen and two Irishmen travelled regularly to work on the same train. After a while it became apparent to the Irishmen that the two Englishmen only had one ticket between them and on enquiring how they managed to achieve this, they explained that when the conductor was heard approaching from the other end of the carriage, the two of them left their seats, went into the toilet and locked the door. When the conductor knocked on the door of the toilet saying, 'Tickets please', they pushed one ticket under the door, which was duly stamped and pushed back under the door again.

The Irishmen thought this was a very good idea and the following morning bought one ticket between them, only to find that in their usual carriage there was only one Englishman. They told him what they had done and also told the Englishman that they presumed he must have a ticket as he was travelling on his own.

He said he did not have a ticket at all and in answer to their enquiry as to how he proposed to manage to travel free of charge, he told them they would have to wait and see what happened when the conductor arrived.

As soon as the conductor was heard approaching, the two Irishmen immediately went to the toilet and locked the door.

A few moments later the Englishman followed them down the corridor and knocked smartly on the toilet door saying, 'Tickets please'.

One Irish ticket appeared under the door.

At first glance...

Here's a trump to make you feel warm. The *New York Times* reported in 1969 that a conservatively-dressed man who boarded the subway at the Times Square station was the victim of a strange assault.

As he stepped into the carriage a weird-looking youth with frizzy hair stuck his foot in the door, preventing the train from leaving. Pointing at the gentleman he screamed over and over again, 'Give me back my yo-yo!'.

The gentleman maintained a dignified silence. The youth continued yelling. Finally, another passenger, announcing that he had to get to work, pushed the deranged youth's foot away. The doors closed and the train pulled out of the station. The rest of the passengers relaxed.

Just as the train stopped at the next station, the gentleman reached into his coat pocket and, smiling enigmatically, stepped out onto the platform spinning a large, red yo-yo.

Show me the way to go home

Mrs Milly Stanton of Meltham, Yorkshire, hated shopping in Huddersfield. There was always too much traffic. The streets were jammed with people and she could never find what she wanted in the shops. What really got her back up were the drivers at the end of the working day. On several occasions she'd had to run off a zebra crossing because an approaching car had kept on going and once it was only a passer-by grabbing her arm and pulling her back that stopped her from being flattened by a maniac overtaking on the inside of a busy road. Mrs Stanton declared war on the drivers of Huddersfield and went into battle shortly after her close escape.

Choosing a bus route that she didn't normally use the good lady got herself to the front of a long queue at a bus-stop on a damp, cold evening when the shops were shutting and the evening traffic was building up. When the bus arrived she stepped in and put her bags down beside her so that no one else could get on board. Then she took a pad of paper from her pocket, fished a pencil out of her handbag and started to write in large letters: 'DOES THIS BUS GO TO THE STATION?' The driver realized that he had a deaf mute at the head of the queue and shook his head vigorously.

Mrs Stanton kept her nerve and wrote on the pad: 'WHERE CAN I GET A BUS THAT DOES GO TO THE STATION?'

The poor driver knew that it would be more than his job was worth to throw a disabled passenger off the bus into the dark, wet night. So with the greatest patience in the face of angry passengers and furious hooting from the cars behind, he carefully wrote directions for the handicapped lady so that she could catch her bus to the station. When he finished she read the instructions through very slowly and then wrote: 'THANK YOU', before she got off the bus, remembering to leave her bags behind so that she would have to fight her way back through the queue once again to retrieve them.

She estimated that the traffic stretched back for a good half-mile when she walked down the pavement beside it and she felt a great sense of triumph when she looked at the drivers staring out of their windows or even getting out of their cars to see what was causing the hold-up. She felt a twinge of guilt about her unwitting accomplice, the bus driver, who had been so kind and helpful. So, having taken a note of his number, that evening she sent off a letter of thanks to the manager of the bus station to tell him how thoughtful the man had been. Out of modesty she didn't give the name or address of the deaf-and-dumb lady he had helped.

Hit and run

I always say, if you're going to produce an excuse, make it as far-fetched as you can – though if your version of the truth is even stranger than fiction, that's even better.

When the police patrol car screamed past him on the A1 with its lights flashing, its red *Stop* sign illuminated and with the loud-speaker telling him to pull over, Mr Arthur Haynes, from Castleford, Yorkshire, complied. The policemen both got out and while one of them came to the driver's window, the other started examining the suspicious-looking dent in the bonnet and front offside wing of Mr Haynes's Hillman Avenger.

'We've had a report of a hit-and-run case near Pontefract involving a car fitting this description and seen heading for the north-bound carriageway of the North Road,' the policeman at the window told Mr Haynes. 'Your car fits the description. You're heading north on the road in question. There's a socking great dent in the front and not a spot of rust on the bare metal, which means it's very recent. What've you got to say about it?'

'An elephant sat on it in Doncaster,' said Mr Haynes.

'Oh yes?' said the officer. 'Fetch one of the bags, Ted,' he called to his mate. 'This gentleman says he's been sat on by an elephant.'

'I'd just like you to blow into this,' he said when he was given the breathalyser, 'then I think we'll be asking you to come with us to the station.'

'Take a look at this, if you don't believe me,' said Mr Haynes waving a sheet of paper in front of the officer.

It was an insurance claim form signed by the manager of the circus that was leaving Doncaster when Mr Haynes had driven up behind it, admitting liability for the damage to the car. Apparently Mr Haynes had slowed down behind the elephant and was keeping a respectable distance when the animal stopped abruptly, took the weight off its feet and sat down on Mr Haynes's car.

The policeman looked a bit put out, but told Mr Haynes to get the car fixed as quickly as he could and let him go. It was just as well he hadn't blown into the bag. Mr Haynes had needed several drinks in Doncaster to get over the shock!

Mystery tour

As you may have gathered, I don't like flying at the best of times. Spending part of my holiday in dreadful anticipation, cooped up in the airport, is my idea of a living hell. Apart from anything else I'd be tempted to get so smashed that I wouldn't even make it to the plane when it was time to leave.

OK, Harry Wells knew that there were going to be long delays because of the air-traffic controllers' strike, but he didn't expect to spend two days sitting on his backside in the departure lounge at Gatwick. Nor did he expect the airline to care so little about what happened to him and his family. When they eventually did take off to Barcelona he felt too relieved to do anything except join in the general rejoicing.

However, towards the end of his fortnight in the sun, he started thinking about the flight home and the horror that that might involve. He concluded that even if the flight home was uneventful, the least he could do would be to put the airline to some inconvenience as a mark of revenge.

Harry borrowed a typewriter from the hotel he was staying in and spent an hour typing out a flight schedule giving details of altitude, speed, weather and estimated time of arrival. He thought it looked pretty authentic by the time he'd finished and he doubted if any of the holidaymakers, who only flew once a year anyway, would be able to tell it from the real thing.

As they took off Harry took out his flight schedule and dropped it in the gangway behind him so that the passenger sitting behind could see it and pick it up. At the head of the sheet was the instruction to pass it on to the man sitting behind her. The sheet had been on the move for about five minutes when a commotion started towards the back of the cabin and people began calling for the stewardesses who were busy trying to serve coffee and sell duty-free goods. Within minutes the place was in uproar and if the plane could have been brought to a halt in mid-take-off it would have been. All the passengers were in a great state of alarm at having embarked on the wrong flight. Harry's schedule showed that they were en route for Buenos Aires via the Azores.

Emergency stop

Vintage car enthusiast, Bill Courtenay, of Winsford, Cheshire, owned one of the few surviving Model T Fords in the neighbourhood. Bill was justly proud of this car and he used to enjoy driving it to work each day. Once on the way home he was stopped by an over-enthusiastic policeman who gave the car a thorough examination. When he couldn't find anything wrong with the car when it was stationary, the policeman told Bill that he wanted to see how it handled on the move. He told him to drive along at a steady 30mph and to do an emergency stop as soon as he heard the policeman sound his horn.

Bill knew that his brakes were tip-top and he decided to teach the copper a lesson. He drove perfectly for a mile-and-a-half and when he heard a loud hooting right on his tail he shoved his foot down hard on the brakes. There was a violent crash at the back of the car and Bill's beloved Model T fell apart. Bill's trump had, as it were, backfired. It wasn't the police car that had hooted.

RULES OF HOWERD

1) The number of transport staff in sight at any given time will be in inverse proportion to:
   a) their willingness to help passengers
   b) their knowledge of the timetable
   c) the number of trains arriving and departing

2) When flying for business meetings the weather will be perfect, the flight will leave on time and you'll lose the contract. When flying for your annual fortnight's holiday, the weather will be stiflingly hot as you sit in the departure lounge in Luton or Manchester; when you arrive in Malaga they'll be having the first rain of the summer; the aircraft will be double-booked on your return and your package ticket will exclude you from compensation; and you will find yourself sitting next to a passenger who's sick even before they shut the door for take-off.

3) Obeying speed limits only helps when there are police cars around to catch you. The likelihood is that you'll be caught on the only occasion when you let the needle creep over thirty.

4) It is more natural for a piece of machinery to be static than moving. Therefore we should be more surprised when the car goes than when it doesn't.

11

Bizasters

(or No Trumps!)

'The best laid schemes o'mice an' men gan aft a-gley,' wrote good old Robert Burns.

And by way of conclusion, to breathe a chilling air of reality, here are just a few of the bizasters encountered by a few hapless individuals to which there were no answers or ways of escape – no trumps, in fact.

Bizasters? Yes, disasters so appalling and bizarre that the only possible outcome is to admit defeat and hotfoot it before the worst happens, content to let Dame Fate blow a giant raspberry in your face.

And just to set the ball rolling, as it were, here's one of the many little mishaps that had me running for my life.

Through a series of unfortunate misunderstandings I found myself one morning in Belgium at the end of the war in the role of military interpreter. The major I was with didn't speak a word of French, and I only had a smattering. So between us we didn't do much for the Allied war effort as we made our way through one small village, trying, in all innocence, to locate expectant mothers and allocate their extra milk ration.

I'd spent several hours carefully preparing my one sentence in French which (even though it was strictly accurate, as I was later told) went something like: 'Nous voulons savoir si une femme voudrait avoir un enfant' –

which I reckoned was unfussy, but polite at the same time. How wrong could I be!

I tried this sentence out on several of the women-folk with a mixed response. Some just looked bored. Others took mild offence and the rest fled for their lives. One woman fetched her husband, who looked like a one-man platoon. I took one look at the pitchfork in his hand and decided the time had come to beat a dignified retreat. The major agreed with me and we both hightailed it out of the village before the villagers helped us on our way.

And my problem? A simple grammatical slip-up, that's all. Instead of asking whether any woman in the village was going to have a baby, I'd innocently suggested that some of them might want to have a baby... Well, it's a mistake anyone could have made... isn't it? By the number of children running around I reckon quite a few mistakes had been made in that village.

Showbiz

I may have done some pretty odd things in the name of showbiz in my time – I still reckon the episode with the parachute harness takes the biscuit, unless it was appearing at the matinée in Streatham in my wellies and pyjamas because I'd overslept (but that's another story), but at least I've stayed clear of goings-on like this one...

In a gallant gesture to raise money for the Variety Club of Great Britain a Grimsby night-club manager named Brian Cottingham, decided to jump the 37 feet from the top of the pier at Cleethorpes. The only omission from his carefully-laid plans, which included a crash helmet and a pair of water-wings, was a glance at the tide-tables. When Mr Cottingham arrived at the end of the pier he found that the sea was about three-quarters of a mile away.

Not wishing to disappoint the large crowd that had gathered to watch him perform his daring feat, the intrepid Mr Cottingham took a deep breath, waved to the

crowd, yelled 'The show must go on' and, in the best traditions of showbiz, jumped.

From his hospital bed he issued a statement that he had been very pleased to see so many people turning up to watch his heroic leap. But, of course, he knew the old showbusiness maxim – 'get off while they still want you' – and that's why he wouldn't do an encore.

Watch your fingers

A few years ago *The Times* reported that dustman George Stevenson was pushing new refuse sacks through front doors one morning in Buckhorpe when he felt one of the sacks being grabbed fiercely as soon as he'd pushed it through the letter-box. Something inside him told him to hang on. He did and a mighty tug-of-war began.

As the sack was jerked inside the house Mr Stevenson

pulled on it for all he was worth and the contest moved one way and then the other until Mr Stevenson felt his strength giving way. He called out to his mate, David Lifer, to give him a hand and soon the two dustmen were engaged in a life-or-death struggle to stop the sack from disappearing through the letter-box. They'd got a good grip on the plastic when they suddenly felt the puller on the inside relax. The two men instantly gave a mighty heave, and shot backwards. At the same time the front

door was ripped off its hinges and landed on top of them. When they looked up to see what they had been struggling with they saw a crocodile with the other end of the refuse bag in its jaws. It turned out in court that the tenant had trained his pet crocodile to carry the morning paper upstairs each day.

In deep water

When the local skin-diving club returned to Penzance from their diving trip to the Highlands of Scotland none of the members could honestly refer to their trip as an unqualified success. Mind you, anyone who gets a thrill out of dressing up in those latex pyjamas and swimming in murky water needs their heads looking at for a start. Though when I hear about all that treasure lying there – valuable if somewhat damp – I'm tempted to have a go myself.

Anyhow the Penzance club had arranged to dive in Scotland's beautiful Loch Buidhe and the members had travelled the 700 miles north in eager anticipation of water as clear as gin, underwater life they had never seen before – and pubs that never closed.

The setting certainly lived up to their expectations and everyone was quickly changing into diving gear before the inaugural plunge beneath the surface. That was where the trouble started. None of the divers could actually get underwater. One of the statistics about Loch Buidhe which had been overlooked in the enthusiasm to dive in Scotland was that it is less than a foot deep.

A note of triumph

If you make a regular practice of bashing your car into parked cars while there are crowds of witnesses looking on to prove your guilt, telling the truth can have its drawbacks after a while. It can lose you a No Claims bonus and cost you a bomb in repairs to your own car.

One way to avoid this is to stop driving. Another is to bend the rules a bit, like the famous story of the American motorist who left a note tucked behind the windscreen-wiper of the parked car he had just run into. The unfortunate owner of the wrecked car returned some time later and picked up the note.

'I have just run into your car', it read. 'People have seen me and are watching me write this. They think I am giving you my name and address. They are wrong.'

The Revenger's Tragedy

The story goes that the doubting husband earned his living driving loads of premixed concrete around the Home Counties. His work took him miles from home and often he was not back until well into the evening. He'd been having doubts about his wife for some time when one job took him near his own home in the middle of the day and he decided to check up on her and catch her in the act, to see if she was really being unfaithful to him or not and if she was – to catch her at it – if I may be so forthright.

As he passed his house he looked up to the first floor and saw that the bedroom curtains were drawn. He also saw a gleaming sports car parked outside the house. Furious with jealousy the cuckold (good word that) turned into a side street until he figured out what to do.

Five minutes later he backed his lorry up behind the sports car. Furtively he rigged up the chute from the back of the lorry, positioned it over the open cockpit of the sports car and proceeded to fill it with concrete. As soon as the level of the concrete in the car had risen to the top of the seats the driver shut off the flow, jumped into his cab and started off down the road. As he was waiting to turn into the main road at the top, he glanced in his rear-view mirror and saw a man come out of his house and walk up to the sports car. Ignoring the traffic the driver watched him strap a crash helmet onto his head and then ride off down the road on a moped parked in front of the sports car.

Marooned

Frank Dixon and his wife Cynthia were driving late through the night to meet up with their daughter and son-in-law in their holiday camp-site in southern France. They were towing a caravan and as the back of the car was full of suitcases and other luggage Cynthia said that she wanted to sleep in the caravan. It was dark. They were miles from any large town and there wasn't much chance of being stopped by the police. So Frank stopped and Cynthia climbed into her bunk for the night. Three hours later Frank stopped again to have a pee. This woke up Cynthia who took the opportunity of nipping into the field to do the same thing. She was squatting down behind a tree when to her horror she heard the car start up and drive away without her.

The first thing Frank knew about it was when he pulled into a petrol station to fill up and looked in the caravan to see how Cynthia was. By now she was forty miles away wandering beside a deserted road in her nightie without a clue where she was.

After my few close shaves with midnight breakdowns my heart goes out to this poor soul. But at least I had the advantage of being properly dressed and being able to speak the lingo.

A loyal toast

Not long after the happy news that the Prince of Wales was going to marry Lady Diana Spencer one loyal subject of the crown, a Scottish businessman named Peter Balfour had the pleasure of congratulating the lucky prince in person. Not content with that, he wished to extend the greetings of everyone present at the meeting to the happy couple and, raising his glass, he asked them to join him in drinking the health and happiness of 'Prince Charles and Lady Jane'!

So don't go searching the Honours List for his name.

Visitation from above

Eager to encourage his congregation to sing with greater enthusiasm the Rev Yeomans of Pontesbury, Shropshire,

left his accustomed position during the service and began to dance in the aisles, waving his arms above his head and lending his own inimitable stamp to the worship of the Lord.

As the voices in the church were raised in appreciation of his lead the vicar became even more energetic in his movements, but as if in protest at this sudden disturbance the floor gave an awesome creak and seconds later the vicar was lying in the crypt next to the boiler staring bewilderedly at a large hole in the floor-boards above. One gathers, as we say in showbiz, that 'it went down well'. Of course, the church wardens found it all most unseemly until they saw the size of the collection. Then they started planning what he could do as an encore.

Mirror, mirror on the wall

The nearest I came to having a face-lift was when I got involved in an altercation with some brute during my club act. I've been told so often that my face resembles that of a weary old camel that I toyed with the idea of having something done to it. At least I thought I might look like a weary *young* camel. But this tale put me off.

Vanity can have its problems, as one middle-aged patient discovered to her cost after she underwent plastic surgery to iron out a few of life's creases in her face. A plastic surgeon advised filling her frown-line with liquid silicone. The operation was duly performed and the patient made a speedy and pleasing recovery. She felt several years younger. Then calamity struck.

Waking up one morning she felt out of sorts and went to look at herself in the mirror. To her horror she saw a ghoulish mask staring back at her. The liquid silicone had shifted from its intended site and had lodged in other recesses of her face. She now saw that her nose stretched right across her eyelids and was an inch wider than before round her nostrils.

No, don't mock...it isn't funny...poor soul.

Radio interference

When things start going wrong with your body, kindly people often try to cheer you up by telling you not to worry, because there's nothing seriously wrong. Usually they haven't a clue what they're talking about, but not infrequently, they're right. But if you'd been a friend of the next case, how would you have gone about cheering him up?

Fears of incontinence plagued one male resident of a seaside nursing home when he found himself suddenly passing water for no explicable reason. He reported his worries to the medical staff and they told him to keep an accurate record of when this alarming event took place.

After keeping a careful check of his bladder action over several months the doctors realized that his sudden releases coincided with the launching of the local lifeboat. Apparently the electronic emptying device that controlled the patient's partially paralysed bladder operated on exactly the same wavelength as the lifeboat's radio.

Knife in the back

Surely this bizaster takes the biscuit? An American was sitting at a bar one evening when a man came up behind him and stabbed him in the back. Just managing to turn round to face the assailant, he noticed a look of horror cross his face. 'I'm so sorry', said the attacker, 'I thought you were someone else.' Oops!

RULES OF HOWERD

'Better be wise by the misfortunes of others than by your own' – Aesop. Hear, hear.